# Guide to the Unconscious

# Guide to the Unconscious

NATALINO CAPUTI

Religious Education Press
Birmingham, Alabama

**Library of Congress Cataloging in Publication Data**

Caputi, Natalino.
  Guide to the unconscious.

  Includes bibliographical references and index.
  1. Subconsciousness.   I. Title.
BF315.C27   1984         154.2         83-24620
ISBN 0-89135-042-X

Religious Education Press, Inc.
1531 Wellington Road
Birmingham, Alabama 35209
10 9 8 7 6 5 4 3 2

Religious Education Press publishes books exclusively in religious
education and in areas closely related to religious education. It is
committed to enhancing and professionalizing religious education
through the publication of serious, significant, and scholarly works.

PUBLISHER TO THE PROFESSION

## DEDICATION

I dedicate this book to my father Uldino and my mother Eleonora, both of whom had the faith in me and in what I was doing to provide the time and place and, most importantly, the unconditional support to see this work to its completion. I also want to acknowledge the emotional support given to me by my wife Judy. It was her companionship that provided the sweetness in the otherwise hard, long, and lonely work of writing this book.

# Contents

# Preface

This book began with a personal question. I was curious about what the unconscious is. The construct had for me an air of mystery about it. It seemed though that the more I read about the unconscious the more confused I got. The various writers were using the expression "the unconscious" in their own particular way. It seemed that each theorist was inventing a new type of unconscious. I soon realized that the book that I was hoping to read did not exist. The topic of the unconscious does not have a basic text. The books that were suggested to me were really partial treatments of the topic. I decided that I would write the very book that I was hoping to read. So, what began as a personal matter developed into a desire and plan to make a contribution to the field of study regarding the topic of the unconscious.

I began the investigation with another question, this time an academic one rather than a personal one, namely, what are writers referring to when they use the construct of the unconscious? The construct means different things to different people. It is an idea which is many times surrounded with an air of importance, yet shrouded in confusion, controversy, and mystery. The unconscious has been described with a motley array of images, adjectives, and prefixes and entangled in many philosophical questions.

There have been efforts to clarify the topic, but they tended to be small-scaled and limited. What is proposed in this book is a comprehensive, four-factor typology that can function as an ordering principle for the many ideas regarding the unconscious. Indeed, typology proves to be an adequate enough way to make sense of the universe of discourse about the unconscious. Despite the usual liabilities of a typological approach such as artificiality, misrepresentation, and omission, it is a necessary first step in facilitating a better understanding of the unconscious.

It was discovered after surveying a major portion of the literature that there are fundamentally four approaches toward the understanding of the unconscious, and each approach centers around one identifiable type of unconscious. These four approaches I have designated as the Bio-Physical, Psycho-Personal, Socio-Cultural, and Transpersonal-Spiritual. The Bio-Physical Approach involves a type of unconscious that is related to the subtle processes that are a function of our physical body. The Psycho-Personal Approaches involves an unconscious that is essentially derived from and a function of one's personal emotional and cognitive development. The Socio-Cultural Approach involves a type of unconscious that is a function of some collectivity, as for example, a racial unconscious. The Transpersonal-Spiritual Approach involves an unconscious that is conceived of as a substantive, transpersonal entity or as a medium to contact transpersonal entities.

Within each approach area the respective theorists are identified. What has resulted is a virtual catalogue of people and ideas centering on the topic of the unconscious. Altogether this collection represents the broadest context within which the topic of the unconscious has been presented and discussed. Besides compiling the first extensive typology on the topic of the unconscious, I have in the process assembled a comprehensive body of statements about the little-known and subtle factors that influence human behavior. Most importantly I have answered the opening question, namely, what are writers referring to when they use the construct of the unconscious.

I wish to express my appreciation to Nelson Thayer for his perseverance in reading and critiquing the various drafts for both style and content. I am also grateful to Thomas Oden for the encouragement he gave me from the beginning that this investigation of the unconscious would be a valuable contribution. I am indebted to Edward Domber, who, due to his expertise as a physiological psychologist, was able to ensure that the second chapter is an adequate representation of the bio-physical approaches.

A special note of thanks to the staff of the Rose Library at Drew University. They were indispensible in the nuts and bolts researching of this book.

NATALINO CAPUTI

# Chapter I

# Introduction

## The Importance of the Topic of the Unconscious

What is "the unconscious"? Is it a force, a field, a process, an entity, a being, a system, or a realm of the mind? Is it only an abstract, collective word, a *nomen* rather than a *res?* If it is the latter, a "thing," is it a positive, negative, or neutral "thing"? Are we to coax it, cultivate it, come to terms with it, trust it, obey it, fear it, conquer it, make it conscious, or keep it unconscious? All of these options have been suggested. If the unconscious is no "thing," what is meant when the expression is used? It has, in fact, been used within the broadest variety of subject areas. The construct of the unconscious has appeared in the literature of psychology, philosophy, sociology, art, literary studies, religious studies, education, anthropology, creativity, and so forth. The expression "the unconscious" has functioned like a Rorschach inkblot in that it has meant different things to different people. No matter how the construct of the unconscious is used, though, there is an unmistakable air of importance surrounding it. Just how important it is will be revealed by the following comments.

These comments have been gleaned from the literature and represent either extracts or paraphrases of what writers have articulated about what they thought was the importance of the construct of the unconscious. They have said that:

The discovery of unconscious states is the most important step forward in psychology. William James, *The Varieties of Religious Experience* (London: Longmans, Green, and Co., 1923), p. 233.

Human behavior cannot be understood without understanding the unconscious aspect. Ner Littner, "Usefulness of Psychoanalytic Theory, Discussion," *Smith College Studies in Social Work* 37, no. 2 (1967), p. 1.

No psychological theory can do without it. Howard Shevrin and Scott Dickman, "The Psychological Unconscious, a Necessary Assumption for all Psychological Theory?" *American Psychologist* (May 1980), p. 432.

It is *the* problem of psychology and any theory which ignores it is false. Gustave Geley, *From the Unconscious to the Conscious* (New York: Harper & Brothers, 1920), p. 84.

To explore the most sacred depths of the unconscious will be the principal task of psychology in the century which is opening. Henri Bergson, quoted in Lancelot Whyte, *The Unconscious Before Freud* (New York: Basic Books, 1960), p. 181.

The problem of the unconscious is *the* problem of psychology. Sigmund Freud, *The Standard Edition of the Complete Psychological Works of Sigmund Freud,* ed. James Strachey, vol. 5: "The Interpretation of Dreams" (London: Hogarth Press, 1974), p. 611.

The concept of the unconscious has long been knocking at the gates of psychology and asking to be let in. Sigmund Freud, *The Collected Papers of Sigmund Freud,* ed. James Strachey, vol. 5: "Some Elementary Lessons in Psychoanalysis" (New York: Basic Books, 1959), p. 382.

The ultimate purpose of the concept is to link conscious awareness and behavior with its background. Lancelot Whyte, "Unconscious," *Encyclopedia of Philosophy,* ed. Paul Edwards (New York: Macmillan and Free Press, 1967), p. 185.

One of the most complex problems facing the sciences dealing with human nature. F. Bassin and A. Sherozia, "The Role of the Category of the Unconscious in the System of the Present-Day Scientific Knowledge of the Mind," paper presented at the International Symposium on the Problem of the Unconscious, Tbilisi, USSR in 1979, p. 1.

It is impossible to understand human behavior, creativity, and psychosomatics without having studied the unconscious. Leon Chertok, "Reinstatement of the Concept of the Unconscious in the Soviet Union," *American Journal of Psychiatry* 138, no. 5 (1981), pp. 581–82.

To ignore the unconscious is to become a victim of inner forces. Sonia Riha, "The Unconscious and Symbolic Imagery," unpublished doctoral dissertation, California School of Professional Psychology, 1972, p. ix.

In the penal system, the concept may decide the fate of a man's life; people change occupations, choose a new spouse, maim their children, worship their God, fight wars "because" of it. Mark Conkling, "Sartre's Refutation of the Freudian Unconscious," *Review of Existential Psychology and Psychiatry* 8, no. 2 (1968), p. 86.

It is the source of mathematical imagination, the hypothesis of the scientist, inspiration of the poet, and the intuition of the everyday man. C. M. Child, ed., *The Unconscious, A Symposium* (New York: Alfred A. Knopf, 1927), p. 1.

It houses the possibility of psychic control over matter. Frank Haronian, "A Psychosynthetic Model of Personality and Its Implication for Psychotherapy," *Journal of Humanistic Psychology* 15, no. 4 (Fall 1975), p. 51.

With it, one has the power to turn his desires into realities. Charles Bristol, *The Magic of Believing* (New York: Pocket Books, 1948), cover words.

We would be fools not to investigate the predictive powers of the unconscious. It is directly related to today's USA-USSR power struggle. David Loye, *The Knowable Future* (New York: Wiley, 1978), pp. 125–26.

It is important for the twentieth century theologian to know about it if he wants to be able to reach the man of the twentieth century. Carl Jung in Victor White, *God and the Unconscious* (London: Harvill Press, 1952), p. xxv.

No other single factor is today so fraught with good or evil, with potential benefit or disaster for mankind. Lancelot Whyte, *The Unconscious Before Freud* (New York: Basic Books, 1960), p. 9.

Science, psychosomatic medicine, and education will suffer if the idea is ignored. F. Bassin and A. Sherozia in Stanley Krippner, *Human Possibilities: Mind Exploration in the USSR and Eastern Europe* (Garden City, New York: Anchor Press/Doubleday, 1980), p. 194.

To examine, learn about it, and deal with it is important for planetary survival . . . this is on the level of a moral and biological imperative. Morton Kelsey, *Dreams: A Way to Listen to God* (New York: Paulist Press, 1978), pp. 237–38.

The psyche of man is the most dangerous thing in the world. Carl Jung, "Does the World Stand on the Verge of Spiritual Rebirth," *C. G. Jung Speaking,* ed. W. McGuire and R. Hull (Princeton: Princeton University Press, 1977), pp. 67–75.

Woe to the age which violently suppresses its voice. Eduard von Hartmann, *The Philosophy of the Unconscious* (London: Routledge & Kegan Paul, 1950), p. 42.

In sum, we see that the construct of the unconscious is felt to be significant for psychology, the individual, and the world. This is an impressive list of how people have interpreted the importance of the construct. There are few other subjects of which one can read so many strong and rather dramatic statements. There is not only a sense of importance conveyed by these comments, but also a decided sense of urgency surrounding the construct. At this point, we will let the literature speak for itself. In the concluding sections of this book, we will reevaluate the importance of the construct of the unconscious.

## The Confusion About the Unconscious

Now that we have seen evidence of how important the topic of the unconscious seems to be, we want to present evidence of how confused the subject matter really is. We will do this by distinguishing three things: 1) the confusion of images; 2) the confusion of neologisms; and 3) the confusion of issues surrounding the construct.

When the expression "the unconscious" is used, it is often used as if the reader understands what is being referred to or that there is only one understanding of it—the author's. As a result of these misunderstandings, there is little effort on the part of the writer to define terms. As will soon become evident, it is not only a problem of one word with many meanings, but also a problem of many words (neologisms) and many meanings. The result of this is a confusion of words and conceptualizations and confusions in discussions. It is the purpose of this book to declare explicitly this state of confusion, and to introduce an ordering principle, namely the typology, which will make sense of the vast literature on the topic. In the end, we will be able to get a better reading (literally) on what the construct of the unconscious is referring to.

Few people actually realize the magnitude of the problem of confusion to which we have alluded to. It is the purpose of the subsequent presentations to portray the exact proportions of the problem. We have made use of three lists. All the items in the lists were taken from the literature, and, assembled in one place, form interesting montages of images and nuances of meaning.

First to be presented is a list of images that try to picture what the unconscious is like. The unconscious has been imaginatively conceived of in terms of the following:

2,000,000 year old man within us
The Invisible Man
Cosmic computer
Storehouse of memories
Storehouse of the wisdom of the ages
Womb
Black hole
Eternally, living, creative, germinal layer
Executor of plans
Field or dark field
Universal creative field
Force or power
Hibernating beast

Steam-kettle
Underworld
Terra incognita
Interior Africa
Shadow of the mind
Cellar of the mind
Seething cauldron
Reservoir of energy
Dark continent
Buried strata of the psyche
Inner devil that cannot be cast out
The demon within
New continent
Augean Stables
Factory
The ghost
Penumbral zone
Internal guru
Guardian angel
Faithful secretary
Tireless, receptive plate
Twilight zone
Sleeping soul
It
The other me
Mother Lode

Added to this list of metaphors is this list of analogies:

Conscious is to the unconscious, as Jekyll is to Hyde.
Conscious is to the unconscious, as an island is to the ocean.
Conscious is to the unconscious, as a spire is to the cathedral.
Conscious is to the unconscious, as the tip of an iceberg is to the rest of the iceberg.

These images, by themselves, reflect the sense of importance, urgency, plurality, and confusion surrounding the construct of the unconscious. Can or how can the unconscious be so many different, and sometimes conflicting things? There is no sense that these images are referring to the same thing. There is an interesting mixture here of positive, negative, and neutral images. One can now understand why the comment was made that "the history of the philosophy and the psychology of the 'unconscious' appears to be nothing more than the history of picturesque and fantastic, not to say grotesque figures of speech."[1]

Now that we have seen the many images conjured up to describe the unconscious, let us consider the different neologisms that have been coined to distinguish the unconscious. As will soon become evident, there is a wide and wild market trafficking in names for the unconscious. Again, these have all appeared in the literature. Only names presented alphabetically will be given to identify the originator of particular neologisms. The list of neologisms for the unconscious include the following:

| | |
|---|---|
| Lower Unconscious | |
| Middle Unconscious | Roberto |
| Higher Unconscious (or Superconscious) | Assagioli |
| Collective Unconscious | |
| | |
| Physiological Unconscious | Leopold |
| Configurational Unconscious | Bellak |
| | |
| Physiological Unconscious | |
| Perceptive Unconscious | Donald |
| Apperceptive Unconscious | Brinkmann |
| Vital Unconscious | |
| | |
| General Absolute Unconscious | |
| Partial Absolute Unconscious | Carl |
| Relative Unconscious | Carus |
| | |
| Latent-Consciousness | |
| Subordinate-Consciousness | |
| Fringe-Consciousness | Tanenari |
| Marginal-Consciousness | Chiba |
| Proper-Consciousness | |

Metaphysical Unconscious
Biological Unconscious                                    Henri
Deep Psychological Unconscious                    Ellenberger
More Accessible Psychological Unconscious
Dynamic Unconscious

Emotional Unconscious                                    James
Rational Unconscious                                       Feibleman

Instinctual Unconscious                                  Victor
Spiritual Unconscious                                       Frankl
Transcendent Unconscious

Preconscious                                                   Sigmund
Unconscious                                                     Freud

Absolute Unconscious                                     Eduard von
Physiological Unconscious                              Hartmann
Relative or Psychological Unconscious

Dynamic Psychological Unconscious             William
Physiological Unconscious                              Herron
Physical Unconscious

Personal Unconscious                                      Carl
Collective Unconscious (Objective Psyche)        Jung

Pristine Unconscious                                       David
Blood-Consciousness                                       Kleinbard
Laurentian Unconscious

Subliminal Unconsciousness
Inattentive Unconsciousness
Insightless Unconsciousness                          James G.
Forgetful Unconsciousness                             Miller
Inherited Unconsciousness
Involuntary Unconsciousness
Incommunicable Unconsciousness

| | |
|---|---|
| Distant or Palingenetic Unconscious | Joseph Montmasson |
| Subliminal-Consciousness<br>Extra-Marginal Consciousness | Frederick<br>Myers |
| Universal Unconscious | Geoffery<br>Osler |
| Coconscious<br>Subconscious<br>Unconscious | Morton<br>Prince |
| Descriptive Unconscious<br>Dynamic Unconscious | Sydney<br>Pulver |
| Pre-Conscious<br>Psychodynamic Unconscious<br>Ontogenetic Unconscious<br>Trans-Individual Unconscious<br>Phylogenetic Unconscious<br>Extra-Terrestrial Unconscious<br>Super-Conscious | Kenneth<br>Ring |
| Innate Unconscious<br>Acquired Unconscious<br>Freudian Unconscious<br>Metaphysical Unconscious | G. K.<br>Sabnis |
| Neurophysiological Unconscious<br>Response Hierarchy Unconscious | Howard<br>Shevrin |
| Cosmic Unconscious | D. Suzuki |
| Subconscious Self | Louis<br>Waldstein |
| Racial Unconscious | William A.<br>White |

Ground Unconscious
Archaic Unconscious
Submergent Unconscious                          Kenneth
Embedded Unconscious                            Wilber
Emergent Unconscious

(Miscellaneous)

Divine Unconscious                    The Deep Mind
Familiar Unconscious                  The Greater Self
Familial Unconscious                  Bioconscious
Dreaming Mind                         Organic Unconscious
Primordial Unconscious                Primary Unconscious
Causal Unconscious                    Impersonal Unconscious
Synchronistic Unconscious             Eastern Unconscious
Teleological Unconscious              Latent Self

What can be said about this condition of so many words coined to define and distinguish the construct of the unconscious? It is obvious that there cannot be so many different unconsciouses. Many of the above expressions are synonyms for one another. For example, the Freudian unconscious, the psychodynamic unconscious, the emotional unconscious, the dynamic psychological unconscious may be considered to have the same meaning generally. On the other hand, some expressions, although appearing to be synonymous, are not. The Freudian use of the word "unconscious" is not the same as the "unconscious" as used by Morton Prince. Also, the physical unconscious of William Herron has no relationship to the biological or physiological unconscious written about by other theorists.

One could conceivably draw up a chart which shows the relationship of meanings between all the neologisms. One has to doubt though the value of such a chart because the great irony in all this is the fact that there is still so much controversy over whether or not *any* unconscious exists at all. Some have argued that the construct of the unconscious is meaningless, that is, tells us nothing. We can add that, given the fact that the construct of "the conscious" itself is still debated, adding the prefix "un" to it cannot hope to fare any better, in fact, it may suffer more misunderstandings because it adds a confusing prefix to an already confused word.

Given all that we have just said, why have so many people derived so many verbal expressions? Most of the individuals involved knew of the controversy surrounding the constructs "conscious" and "the unconscious," yet they saw fit to multiply neologisms. Why? Most of them probably did so precisely for the purpose of clarifying, or so they believed. Again, the irony is that so many efforts to clarify have only resulted in the creation of more confusion. This is so because distinctions offered prematurely, that is, offered before there is any agreement on whether or what is there to distinguish, can only create confusion. If the existence of one unconscious or any unconscious is still debatable, the creation of sixty more names for what is in question does not make it any more substantial. So far the problem of neologisms has been cast in a negative light. On the positive side it is possible that this condition of so many neologisms in a way testifies to the felt importance of what the construct of the unconscious can mean for humanity. In other words, if the unconscious was a topic of little consequence, why would anyone bother to distinguish it so much? These are speculations offered in the attempt to make some sense of the fact of so many words surrounding one word, namely, "unconscious."

The multiplicity of neologisms is just one manifestation of the problem of the unconscious on the level of vocabulary. To compound the problem there are other aspects to consider regarding the word "unconscious." The word has been used as an adjective, an adverb, and as a noun. In the noun form sometimes it appears capitalized as "Unconscious" and sometimes it appears as "The Unconscious." Some authors use all three forms of the word without any attempt to distinguish them.

Another word problem involves the confusion between the terms "subconscious" and "unconscious." Sometimes the words are used as if they mean the same thing and sometimes they are distinguished as referring to two different aspects. It is not uncommon to find both words in the same piece of writing without any distinction made between them. Probably the most extreme example of this type of confusion is Barbara Brown's book *New Mind, New Body.* She used not only the terms "unconscious" and "subconscious," but also "nonconscious" and "subliminal" as if they were interchangeable.

Then there are theorists who prefer one term over another. For example Sigmund Freud, Emil Coue, and Henri Bergson preferred the word "unconscious." They argued that the construct "subconscious" implied a sense of inferiority. On the other hand Charles Baudouin, Pierre Janet, and Morton Prince preferred the word "subconscious." They contended that the word "unconscious" was inconvenient because it applied equally well to purely physiological processes.

If we consider the expressions "subconscious" and "unconscious" on the everyday level, we recognize another nuance of difference. For example, if one were to spot a body lying on the side of the road, one would not say that the person is subconscious, but would use the word "unconscious."

For purposes of researching and presenting this book, although we recognize the differences of opinions regarding the usages of the expressions "subconscious" and "unconscious," we have treated the terms as being synonymous. Some authors, such as Freud and Prince, were careful to distinguish these two words, but most were not so careful. In this book we will use the expression "unconscious" to be consistent and will put the term "subconscious" in parentheses if the author in question made a point of using that expression.

Besides verbal problems regarding the construct of the unconscious, there are philosophical questions related to the implications of the rhetoric surrounding the construct. Abraham Edel made the point that, in the usual controversies about the unconscious, there are almost a dozen issues thoroughly entangled.[2] Those issues involve questions of linguistics, logic, methodology, metaphysics, and psychotherapeutic practice. Philosophers have exercised their expertise to facilitate the ongoing discussion of the question of the unconscious. We will comment on the fruits of their labors in the next section. Here we want to outline some of the questions and answers that have been gleaned from surveying books and articles directly addressing the philosophical issues. For a fuller presentation of the questions and answers, and the appropriate references, Edel's article is excellent. A fuller discussion of some of the issues are integrated within the body of this book. Some of the questions are:

1. Does ordinary language provide a foundation for the use of the word "unconscious"? (As an adjective and an adverb it does, but as a noun, no.)

2. Is the very concept of unconscious ideas and desires self-contradictory? (It depends on one's definition of "ideas" and "desires.")

3. Does the construct of the unconscious involve the acceptance of an entity? (Not necessarily, but many times it seems that way.)

4. Do unconscious mental states exist? (It depends on the definition of "mental.")

5. Can everything that is said in terms of the unconscious be said without it? (Yes, but how adequately depends on who is being asked to accept it.)

6. Are there proofs for the unconscious? (So-called "proofs" are suggestive, but not conclusive.)

7. Does the concept of the unconscious imply the splitting of the mind? (It depends on one's assumptions about mind.)

Entire books, articles, and dissertations have been devoted to the discussion and attempted resolution, refutation, and/or reformulation of these questions and others. The multiplication of such literature has not necessarily increased the understanding of the topic. It is not the intent of this book to reproduce the intricacies of all the arguments. It is the intent, though, of doing a typological investigation to provide a foundation and a broad context for philosophical-critical studies.

To summarize the discussion so far we can say that: 1) the topic of the unconscious seems to be an important one; and 2) it is in a state of confusion on the verbal, imaginal, and philosophical levels. Given these conditions, it is natural to ask how can something, seemingly so important, be so confused? The disparity, between the felt importance and the degree of agreed upon knowledge of the topic, is great. The problems have not gone unnoticed as we shall soon see.

## Previous Efforts to Clarify the Construct of the Unconscious

In the past there have been four forms that efforts to clarify the construct of the unconscious have taken. First, there have been philosophical-critical studies done on the construct. Second, there have been some historical studies done on the idea of the unconscious. Third, there have been some symposiums conducted on the topic. Fourth, there have been some attempts, although small-scale and brief, at a typological approach to the topic. A discussion of these previous efforts, particularly the fourth one, will lead to the introduction of the typology used in this book.

Philosophers and psychologists have attempted to deal critically with some aspect of the problems surrounding the construct of the unconscious. A significant portion of the literature on the topic is precisely devoted to this. But there is an ironical note regarding many of these critical studies. Sometimes the efforts to clarify the construct of the unconscious also tend to add to the confusion. These critiques are needed, but because the subject area on the whole is confused these critiques, which are usually directed to one particular appropriation of meaning regarding the unconscious, may win the battle in that one specific area but lose the war regarding the greater question of the unconscious. For example, a critique of the Freudian understanding of the unconscious may not be relevant to other understandings of the construct or be generalized to include the latter. Critiques make sense within a context. A typological investigation, such as this one, can help place the various worthwhile critiques in the larger context of the topic.

The second major source of efforts to clarify the topic has been the various historical studies that have been done. The most outstanding work was done by Lancelot Whyte with his book *The Unconscious Before Freud*. Whyte conveyed one of the broadest pictures of the vastness of topic of the unconscious existing in the literature at this point. Whyte's work is considered foundational for this book. In a sense, this volume could be entitled "The Unconscious After Freud." As good as Whyte's book is though, it is like other historical treatments; that is, it is incomplete. Probably the best historical work would be one that would incorporate and integrate the specific histories into one body of literature. The construct of the unconscious has surfaced within a variety of traditions in different ways. Historical studies tend to emphasize one tradition or another, hence they are all incomplete. We have yet to see one work on the topic that truly embraces all points of view.

The third form of clarification was in the form of symposiums explicitly convened to discuss the topic of the unconscious. In this century, approximately a dozen such conferences have been held. The last one was in Tbilisi, USSR, in 1979. They have tended to be parochial in the sense that they have treated some aspects of the unconscious or one particular understanding of the topic as if other aspects or points of view did not exist. In 1927 the symposium resulted in a very odd collection of papers that were barely related to one another or to any central theme except that they were bound together in one book under the title "The Unconscious."[3] In short, these symposiums have either been limited in scope or have lacked a context.

The fourth category of efforts to clarify the topic of the unconscious can be considered forerunners of this book. Typology is the method here, but the idea of it, regarding the topic of the unconscious, is not new. There have been three notable attempts.

The earliest attempt at a typological approach was the dissertation, later published book by James G. Miller in 1942, entitled *Unconsciousness*. Miller evaluated the problem of confusion regarding the construct and offered his work as a way to help clarify some of the misunderstandings and ambiguities. He distinguished and discussed sixteen different definitions of what he called "unconsciousness." Those definitions are worth listing here because they are very informative, and we will refer to this list in later sections.

The sixteen definitions are:

1. *inanimate* or subhuman, incapable of discriminating or behaving
2. *absent-minded,* day-dreaming, anesthetized, etc., unresponsive to stimulation
3. *not mental*
4. *undiscriminating*
5. *conditioned,* acting sheerly on the basis of conditioning
6. *unsensing,* for one or more of the following reasons:
    a. stimuli not reaching organism
    b. inadequate stimuli affecting organism
    c. sensory tract incapable of conveying stimuli
    d. subliminal stimuli affecting organism
    e. stimuli not reaching the cortex (or the "seat of awareness" of the nervous system)
7. *unnoticing* or unattending
8. *insightless,* lacking insight in the sense used by the Gestalt school of psychologists
9. *unremembering* due to:
    a. extinction or lack of formation of conditioned response
    b. the wearing away of memories with time
    c. alternative forgetting-incorrect remembering
    d. retroactive inhibition
    e. dissociation
    f. suppression
    g. repression
10. *acting involuntarily*
11. *acting instinctively,* behaving on an unlearned basis
12. *unrecognizing*
13. *unable to communicate*
14. *ignoring*
15. *unaware of discrimination*
16. *psychoanalytic meaning*- dynamically repressed material[4]

Miller suggested that, in order to avoid confusion, these more precise words ought to be used in scientific writing. Miller's book is well-written. He explained in detail his definitions, offered case material as examples of each, and reported on the state of laboratory experimentation regarding each of the areas related to the definitions. It has been said of Miller's work that it is "still the major attempt of the past twenty-five years to define and systematize the concept of the unconscious."[5]

Miller offered his ideas as a way to help bridge the gap between the clinic and the laboratory. He focused his attention solely on the clinical and experimental appropriations of the construct of the unconscious. He did not discuss the more social and transpersonal contexts wherein the construct of the unconscious has been employed by other thinkers to account for certain behaviors. The typology developed in this book will take into account not only the experimental and clinical uses of the construct of the unconscious, but also the social and transpersonal applications of the construct. Although Miller did not do so, that does not mean that some one else could not make use of his definitions for the analysis of behavior in contexts other than the clinic or the laboratory.

A case in point regarding the applicability of Miller's sixteen definitions is the work of Otakar Machotka, a sociologist. Machotka applied the definitions toward the analysis of the unconscious processes and patternings in social relations. Machotka's work is presented in the fourth chapter. Together, Miller's and Machotka's studies are a thorough and detailed description of the many unconscious processes investigated in laboratories, dealt with in the clinic, and found to be operating in social environments. They made their respective analysis without having to speak in terms of the "the unconscious" as, say, Sigmund Freud or Carl Jung did. In other words, Miller and Machotka avoided the noun form usage of the word "unconscious" and employed the adjectival and adverbial forms. They spoke of unconscious processes or processes performed unconsciously, but not of processes carried out by "the unconscious."

The next effort in the direction of a typological approach was done by Henri Ellenberger. That work involved a fifteen-page article at the end of which he considered a certain range of phenomena which have been described under the term "unconscious." He organized them under the following categories:

1. The *metaphysical unconscious:* the "Will" of Boehme, Schelling, Schopenhauer, the "absolute unconscious" of Carus and von Hartmann.

2. The *biological unconscious,* with its formative and organic activity: here belong the "partial absolute unconscious" of Carus, the "physiological unconscious" of von Hartmann, the "Mneme" of Semon, the "psychoid" of Driesch and Bleuler, and "organic unconscious" of Marie Bonaparte. The phenomena of instinct and habit make the transition between this type of unconscious and conscious activity.

3. The *deep psychological unconscious:* the unconscious of the mystics, mesmerists, and parapsychologists, the seat of unconscious creative activity, of the collective symbols (von Schubert, C. Jung).

4. The *more accessible psychological unconscious,* including forgotten memories (Saint Augustine), subliminal perceptions (Leibniz, Herbart, Fechner), "unconscious inference" (Helmholts).

To all these, Freud added a new one: the *dynamic* unconscious of the repressed. Its study had been anticipated by Charcot, Bernheim, Janet, and Flournoy, but almost the whole of it was explored and described by Freud.[6]

Ellenberger's article was a historical study of the idea of the unconscious and his concluding typology was done as a way to summarize his survey. The article is short, but packed with many historical references. His typology is brief, limited in its selection, and small-scaled; but, generally speaking, it corresponds very closely with the one proposed in this book. The major exception here is that Ellenberger did not include what we have called the "Socio-Cultural" type of unconscious.

The final effort at a typological approach that will be considered was done by Lancelot Whyte. We have already cited his work. Like Henri Ellenberger, Whyte was mainly concerned with doing a historical study and only in a secondary way offered a typology.

Whyte in one place presented this interesting list:

### The Unconscious Mind Was Interpreted

| By: | As: |
|---|---|
| Mystics | the link with God |
| Romantics | a divine, universal, plastic principle |
| Early Romantics | the link between the individual and universal powers |
| Post-Romantic Thinker | a factor operating in memory, perception, and ideas |
| Dissociated "Self-Conscious Man" | night: the realm of violence |
| Physical Scientists | the consequence of physiological factors not yet understood |
| Monistic Thinker | the prime mover and source of all order and novelty in thought and action |
| Freud ("Subconscious") | mainly inhibited memories ruled by the pleasure principle, in a state of deformation and conflict, accessible through special techniques |
| Jung | the prerational realm of collective myth and religious symbols[7] |

Whyte, as far as typology is concerned, did not do much more than simply present this list. It is informative, but brief and limited; and, as the title of the book states, it deals with the construct of the unconscious before Sigmund Freud.

Considered separately, the work of Miller, Ellenberger, and Whyte are good beginnings of a more large-scale, comprehensive typological treatment of the topic of the unconscious. Considered together, their works form an impressive body of literature which should be read together in order to get the most complete picture of the vastness of the topic. This book will subsume the work of its forerunners within a comprehensive framework which considers virtually all points of view, and it will bring the topic up-to-date.

## The Typology Developed in this Book

Up to this point, we have presented evidence that the topic of the unconscious is important, that it is in a state of confusion, and that there have been efforts to clarify what is meant by the construct. We also contended that these previous efforts have been limited. It is the intent of this book to be comprehensive and provide future discussion, teaching, and research about the topic of the unconscious the broadest possible context and a reference document.

As a typological inquiry this work is based on identifying, distinguishing, and relating characteristic types of approaches regarding the construct of the unconscious. Even though the literature on the topic is vast and even wild at times, essentially, only one or more of four fundamental types of unconscious are being presented. There are four basic ways of speaking about the unconscious. Defining these ways serves to order the great disparity and variety of opinions, conceptions, and theories about the unconscious. These four ways we have designated as:

1. The *Bio-Physical Approach:* which deals with an unconscious that is related to subtle processes that are a direct function of our physical body.

2. The *Psycho-Personal Approach:* which speaks of an unconscious that is essentially derived from and a function of one's personal emotional and cognitive development. The primary focus here is on such things as memories, feeling, and ideas.
3. The *Socio-Cultural Approach:* the type of unconscious here is understood as a function of some collectivity (e.g. "group mind" or "collective unconscious").
4. The *Transpersonal-Spiritual Approach:* the type of unconscious here is conceived of as some transpersonal entity or as a medium to contact transpersonal entities.

It is the plan of this book to use these four keys to organize and present the various ideas about the topic. We will be able to identify and place much of the literature within one or more of the four approaches. In many ways this is a word study    a study of one word, "unconscious," and how it is used, especially in the expression "the unconscious." We not only want to catalogue the literature, people, and ideas, but also to determine the relevance of the construct and the usefulness of the word "unconscious."

The following comments are offered in the way of helping to avoid misunderstandings regarding the contents of the book. Because a diverse and vast variety of subjects are being subsumed within this study as a typological study, these comments are necessary so that the point is not missed about what is being said about those subjects and/or the people who are presented.

This first point has to do with *what* is presented here. The construct of the unconscious has been associated with many different topics. When we present the discussion of such associations, such as the unconscious and biofeedback, we are not primarily or mainly concerned about biofeedback. There are already many books on just biofeedback. We are mostly concerned that the construct of the unconscious has been related to it. We want to investigate that association and determine if it is necessary, or is it a confusion of two things. The field of biofeedback is vast and the topic of the unconscious is vast. Most of the time they do not overlap. Where they do overlap though is a very confined area. It is that confined area that we are looking into.

This next point has to do with *who* is studied and presented here. It must be emphasized that only those who have explicitly expressed some idea about the unconscious interest us here. Indeed, it has been been precisely those who have made use of the construct who have created the problem of confusion. This point is stressed because, for example, when we consider the "Socio-Cultural Approach," there have been sociologists who have written about the subtle and unofficial processes of a society. But they did not use the construct of the unconscious to articulate their accounts of such things, although they may have used the word "unconscious" as an adjective or adverb. We are interested in those who did use the noun form of the word. Also, it is conceivable that someone could find references and allusions to the idea of the unconscious in almost every philosopher, theologian, and psychologist. But only a much fewer number of them have explicitly used the expression. It is in the latter group that we are interested.

These two points regarding what and who is included in this book have been useful in gathering the material. They have functioned like controls on the literature, which otherwise would be unwieldy and full of temptations to digress.

## Notes

1. S. Daniel House, "Psychologies of the Unconscious," *Psychoanalytic Review* 15 (1928), p. 18.

2. Abraham Edel, "The Concept of the Unconscious: Some Analytic Preliminaries," *Philosophy of Science* 31, no. 1 (1964), pp. 18–33.

3. C. M. Child, ed., *The Unconscious, A Symposium* (New York: Alfred A. Knopf, 1927). For the Russian symposium, see Stanley Krippner's "Problems of the Unconscious," in *Human Possibilities: Mind Exploration in the USSR and Eastern Europe.* (Garden City, New York: Anchor Press/Doubleday, 1980).

4. James G. Miller, *Unconsciousness* (New York: John Wiley & Sons, Inc., 1942), pp. 22–24.

5. Rex Collier, "A Figure-Ground Model Replacing the Conscious-Unconscious Dichotomy," *Journal of Individual Psychology* 20 (1964), p. 3.

6. Henri Ellenberger, "The Unconscious Before Freud," *Bulletin of the Menninger Clinic* 21, no. 3 (1957), p. 14. His other major work on the subject, *The Discovery of the Unconscious,* is a historical study, but more on the history of psychiatry than a history of the idea of the unconscious.

7. Lancelot Whyte, *The Unconscious Before Freud* (New York: Basic Books, Inc., 1960), pp. 72–73.

Chapter II

# Bio-Physical Approach

## Introduction

The first type of unconscious that will be presented is that which emerges out of a bio-physical framework. The expression "Bio-Physical Approach" is used as a generic term to designate that aggregate of literature which discusses the construct of the unconscious as a function of the physical body with its physiological and biological processes. Outside of this aggregate, in the greater bio-physical literature, the word "unconscious" is usually used in its adjectival and adverbial forms. For example, it is usually used to describe some activity that is carried out without awareness, little awareness, or below the normal level of awareness. It is uncharacteristic to find the noun form of the word in such literature. Such usage would imply that some "thing" is being referred to. In the Bio-Physical Approach, we will present those few instances where the noun form is used.

The body of literature composing this approach includes that which discusses, in connection with the construct of the unconscious, memory functions, automatic behavior, conditioning, subliminal events, and the physical foundation of the unconscious. What unites these diverse fields of study is the physical interpretation that they give to the construct. The various neologisms related to the unconscious that have been developed within this approach are:

Lower Unconscious                     Configurational Unconscious
Physiological Unconscious             Perceptive Unconscious
Vital Unconscious                     Organic Unconscious
Instinctual Unconscious               Biological Unconscious

Physical Unconscious            Bioconscious
Neurophysiological             Response-Hierarchy
  Unconscious                    Unconscious[1]

These expressions appear in the literature. Many of them are virtually synonymous. Why authors have coined so many different expressions is sometimes more a mystery than the topic of the unconscious itself.

It is the major contention of this chapter to argue that the construct of the unconscious, particularly in this noun-form usage, has been confused with processes of a bio-physical nature. In other words, phenomena that have been described or explained in terms of some unconscious were really dealing with bio-physical processes and therefore can be described and explained in more parsimonious ways without conjuring up some thing called "the unconscious." To repeat, it is the noun form of the word "unconscious" that is problematic in this approach. The adverbial and adjectival forms of the word are usually not problematic, but even they could be replaced by more descriptive words such as James Miller's sixteen definitions. By making these distinctions, a major source of confusion surrounding the topic of the unconscious is removed.

## Physical Foundation for the Unconscious

There have been those who have investigated the supposed "seat" of consciousness. Some have looked for it through a microscope and others have searched with a scalpel. At various times this "seat" has been located in the liver, stomach, heart, or different areas of the nervous system. In this section of the book, we will present some attempts to locate the "seat" of the unconscious.

According to Gert Heilbrunn, Sigmund Freud in three separate instances expressed his confidence that someday his theories would be substantiated by studies in biology and chemistry.[2] Heilbrunn contended that we have made significant progress in that direction. There have been other studies.

In 1949, Justin Neuman argued for the cerebral cortex as the locus of the unconscious. He distinguished two types of nervous tissue. One is in the service of phylogenetic experiences and the other is in the service of ontogenetic (learned) experiences. The former supposedly represents the Freudian unconscious and is responsible for the symbolic activity in dreams.[3] Neuman wove an obscure and curious blend of anatomical words, Freudian terms, and even some Pavlovian expressions such as the conditioned response.

In 1952, William Calwell suggested that something called the "primitive brain" or "animal mind" in us is the physical basis of the unconscious.[4] This work, like Neuman's, is obscure.

In 1961, Gert Heilbrunn was concerned with the "site or place where the repressed is stored."[5] What he was involved with was the electrical stimulation of certain areas of the brain and the subsequent memories that it activated. He suggested that these areas comprise the unconscious.

In 1966, Geoffrey Osler wrote about the Biologic Brain composed of the thalamus, hypothalamus, and basal ganglia. He speculated that Freud's "Id" could be a conceptual description of the Biologic Brain. Further, Osler suggested that maybe the frontal lobe could be the neurologic substrate of Karen Horney's "Real Self," and that the species-specific stimulus-bound patternings of the Biologic Brain could be related to Jung's notion of the Universal Unconscious.[6] The mood of Osler's article is highly suggestive and speculative only.

In 1967, Conrad Chyatte, Kathleen Mele, and Bonnie Anderson proposed the blood-shift theory that hypothesized a possible physiological basis for repression. The theory suggests that repression is a function of the partial atrophy of unactivated neurons due to receiving low levels of blood nourishment.[7]

The examples just presented represent a few scattered and relatively undeveloped speculations regarding the physical basis of the unconscious. We will now consider some ideas that have emerged out of left-right brain research, which represents a field of study that is organized and developing. In fact, it is becoming more and more popular to speak and think in terms of left and right brain categories. We will first consider the nature of such research as explained by John Eccles, Richard Sperry, Sally Springer, and Georg Deutsch. Then we will look at David Galin's ideas about the implications of such research for the concept of the unconscious. We will also consider the ideas of Rhawn Joseph, who made some speculations based on the study of left-right brain phenomenon.

The following comments, leading up to the experiment that will be cited, are offered as a summary of some of the background information related to this type of brain research.

The human brain is composed of two hemispheres (left and right) linked together mainly by a tract of millions of fibers called the "corpus callosum." Input from the right side of the body is carried to the left hemisphere, and input from the left side to the right hemisphere. The output channels are similarly crossed. The two hemispheres are not identical. They function differently and have different abilities. For example, usually the left hemisphere controls speech. A disconnected right hemisphere cannot express itself verbally, but can express itself through some manual behavior. In normal brain functioning we can say that the two hemispheres share their information, and coordinate their efforts by means of the corpus callosum.

It was found that cutting the corpus callosum, in order to alleviate extreme cases of epileptic seizures, left the patient in a condition referred to as "split-brain." In this condition, the patient exhibited some interesting behavior. Sperry and associates have developed testing procedures in which information can be fed into one or the other hemisphere and in which the responses of either hemisphere can be independently observed. The following experiment is a case in point.

"P.S." [a special "split-brain" subject] was tested with pairs of visual stimuli presented simultaneously to each side of a fixation point located on a projection screen. The picture falling into each visual field was thus processed by the hemisphere normally receiving input from that side of the fixation point. P.S. was asked to use his hands to point to pictures related to what he had seen flashed on the screen from among several placed in front of him. . . . Of particular interest was the way in which P.S. verbally interpreted these double responses: When a snow scene was presented to the right hemisphere and a chicken claw was presented to the left, P.S. quickly and dutifully responded correctly by pointing with the right hand to a picture of a chicken from a series of four cards and, with the left hand, pointed to a picture of a shovel from a series of four cards. The subject was then asked, "What did you see?" "I saw a claw and I picked the chicken, and you have to clean out the chicken shed with a shovel." In trial after trial, we saw this kind of response. The left hemisphere could easily and accurately identify why it had picked the answer, and then subsequently, and without batting an eye, it would incorporate the right hemisphere's response into the framework. While we knew exactly why the right hemisphere had made its choice, the left hemisphere could merely guess. Yet, the left did not offer its suggestion in a guessing vein but rather as a statement of fact as to why the card had been picked.[8]

On the foundation of what has been said so far, and with the experiment just cited in mind, we will consider some speculations based on them.

The first question is "does splitting the brain split the mind?" This type of question has aroused controversy over split-brain studies. Some, such as Richard Sperry, contend that the surgery leaves the person with two distinct minds. Others, such as John Eccles, disagree. The answer to the question depends on two crucial things; that is, what is the criterion to determine that a mind is involved, and how can we be sure that the two hemispheres are completely disconnected? Until we agree on the former and establish the latter, the controversy will continue. So far each side has argued on the foundation of presumptions about the answers to the questions.

The next question is, "What about the feeling of mental unity experienced by patients who have had their corpus callosum cut?" In fact, the patients behave as if nothing at all has been done to them. Specific tests are required to indicate functional disengagement of the hemispheres. What is very interesting here is that back in 1868, Eduard von Hartmann made this observation,

Considerable losses of substances of both hemispheres, or one-sided loss of a whole hemisphere, are sustained by pigeons without permanent change in their behavior, and by rabbits and dogs with a certain loss of intelligence. Even in man total destruction of a cerebral lobe without palpable disturbance has often been observed.[9]

We realize, from this observation by von Hartmann, that the study of phenomena related to brain laterialization is not new. The point here though is that the destruction of a cerebral lobe left the subject relatively unchanged.

Also, if we remember our earlier experiment, one striking feature of it was that the patient's verbal hemisphere constructed (made-up) the reality of what had happened to make sense of its behavior. Such observations have led Sperry, Galin, and others to speculate that perhaps the feeling of mental unity is to some extent an illusion and directly a function of language. Such speculations are highly controversal and loaded with implications, especially regarding the role of language. For example, Michael Gazzaniga and J. LeDoux, who first presented the experiment cited earlier, suggested that the major task of our verbal self is to construct a reality based on our actual behavior without really knowing the origin of some behavior. [10] These considerations lead us to the question: "Can the silent, nondominant hemisphere be considered 'the unconscious'?"

David Galin argued that right brain studies do have implications for the Freudian understanding of the unconscious. Galin pointed out that the right hemisphere's mode of thought is similar to Freud's description of the unconscious, especially regarding the features of nonverbalism, the nonlinear mode of association, and the disregard for time and sequence. Galin hypothesized that,

> In normal intact people mental contents in the right hemisphere can become disconnected functionally from the left hemisphere (by inhibition of neuronal transmission across the cerebral commissures), and can continue a life of their own. This hypothesis suggests a neurophysiological mechanism for at least some instances of repression and an anatomical locus for the unconscious mental contents. [11]

Inhibition of neuronal transmission may be affected by such factors as conflict between the hemispheres, the relatively different histories of reinforcement of each hemisphere's type of response, or that the knowledge that one hemisphere possesses may not translate well into the language of the other. In short, for Galin, the right hemisphere may very well be the physical foundation for the unconscious.

Rhawn Joseph, who did not accept the Freudian model of the unconscious, suggested another line of interpretation based on the findings of brain research. Joseph remarked,

> Language is a relatively late development in one's life . . . much happens to one's life before the right words are attached to those experiences. . . . During these same early years, our traumas, fears, and other emotional experiences were mediated by the silent, nonlinguistic, nondominant cerebral hemisphere as they are in adulthood and processed and stored in a nonverbal prelinguistic code, a code which due to physiological and psychological maturation may become lost to both sides of the brains. Nevertheless, and especially in regards to neurosis, many of these early impressions and feelings remain exactly that; "feelings," present but not identifiable. [12]

With Galin and Joseph we have two views of the right hemisphere. The former sees it in terms of repression, the latter in terms of unverbalized feelings. In the Psycho-Personal Approach, we will discuss in more detail the difference between understanding the unconscious in terms of repression or the unverbalized. For our purposes here, we want to identify Galin and Joseph as two theorists who feel that there is a relationship between the unconscious and the right hemisphere. [13]

There is a certain attractiveness to left-right brain models. Some of these models and certain experiments can be very suggestive and induce various lines of speculations. With Galin and Joseph we saw two examples of this. It is tempting to say, when one considers some unexplainable event or behavior, that they are the function of the right hemisphere. For example, regarding the question of creative inspiration in problem-solving, one can conclude that the left hemisphere formulates the problem and gives it to the right hemisphere to work out, and, when solved, the right hemisphere relays the solution back to the verbal left side. We have to be careful here that we do not reduce everything to either left or right brain categories. As we shall soon point out, the right hemisphere is not the promised land of answers that some have portrayed it to be.

Springer and Deutsch made the point that "ultimately it is likely that dividing the brain in terms of 'where' will not completely answer the question of 'how.' "[14] They were alluding to the classical physical-psychical problem of how to explain the relationship between the two aspects.

There is another question that brain research does not answer, that is, what or who is the agent (if there is an agent) involved, say, when a memory is recalled or an idea emerges? Brain research can point out this or that area of the cerebral cortex and say that it controls speech, hearing, or the memory of certain experiences because the removal or impairment of that area is followed by the inability to speak, hear, or remember something. The logical conclusion is that the area and the function are related, but not that the area caused the function. The area of the brain could have functioned as a facilitator of some event. Springer and Deutsch said something to that effect when they wrote,

> It is likely that most memory impairment consequent to focal brain damage is not so much a removal of localizable "engrams" as an interference with part of the mechanisms or steps involved in forming or retrieving memories.[15]

Given what we have said so far, it is possible that if the constructs such as soul, self, spirit, or spirits refer to entities or beings, then they can have access to the brain (left and right) as a facilitator. This neo-Platonic suggestion is by no means logically excluded by what we have seen of brain research. Brain research, in a sense, represents a recasting of an old problem into new categories (left and right brain). We are referring to the classical dilemma of trying to find the soul of a person with a scalpel. We referred to another expression of this problem in the opening paragraph of this section, that is, the search for the "seat" of consciousness with a scalpel. Today, the technology is relatively advanced and we have more information about the brain, but we have not necessarily advanced our level of understanding about the nature of the human mind. The fundamental questions remain unanswered.

Regarding the search for the physical place for the unconscious, brain research can show that a certain mass of tissue is related to this or that function, but it cannot legitimately declare that that tissue is the unconscious. A certain tissue may be related to phenomena some-times assigned to the construct of the unconscious such as forgotten memories, but such tissue is not necessarily identical with what is meant by the unconscious. To pretend more than this, by those who are anxious to locate the unconscious in the body, is a misuse of the valuable results that have emerged from brain studies. All these things said, there will be those who will continue to search with a scalpel for the "seat" of the unconscious.

We should also mention that there is a problem of criteria involved in postulating that the silent, nonverbal right hemisphere is the unconscious. If one makes consciousness a direct function of the verbal ability of the left hemisphere, then, by definition, the right hemisphere can be designated as the unconscious. D. Galin and R. Joseph have suggested this, but only by their definitions. Someone else, such as Robert Ornstein, may argue that the two hemispheres represent two modes of consciousness rather than one being conscious and the other unconscious. Still another, such as John Eccles, could argue that one cannot speak of the right hemisphere in terms of consciousness except maybe to liken it to animal-type consciousness. In other words, only the left hemisphere can properly be spoken of in terms of consciousness.

Whether brain surgery splits the mind or consciousness, or whether the left and right hemispheres represent two modes of knowledge, two minds, two modes of consciousness, or two persons is ultimately a question of one's definition of mind, consciousness, or person. Up to now, most of the arguments on both sides have been based on certain explicit and/or implicit assumptions.

## The Unconscious Associated with Memory, Biofeedback, Automatic Behavior, Subliminal Perception, and Conditioning

The general plan of this section is to investigate and evaluate the association of the construct of the unconscious with the items listed above.

## MEMORY

The constructs of the unconscious and memory have had a relatively long and close relationship. Ever since the word "unconscious" was coined (mid-eighteenth century) until today, one of the main activities of the unconscious that has been noted is its conservative function, that is, its ability to record and store every experience. This is precisely why the unconscious is referred to as a storehouse. Today though the relationship between the unconscious and memory is held suspect by those who do not accept the construct of the unconscious. In fact, if we say that at one time memory was considered one of the functions of the unconscious, today we can say that reverse, that is, that the unconscious could be considered largely a function of memory systems, processes, and functionings.

This discussion is taken up here under the Bio-Physical Approach because theories of memory have a long history of being based on a physical foundation for memory phenomena. To the extent that the unconscious and memory overlap, the former inherits the physical interpretations assigned to the latter. That which was believed to be retained in memory had been described under various forms, such as, residuum, traces, engrams, or vestiges.[16] Currently, speculations are that RNA, multimolecular proteins, or the synapses between neurons are responsible for memory functioning.[17]

Today, those who research memory processes do not speak in terms of any construct of the unconscious. Confusion between the unconscious and memory usually comes from some who entertain a construct of the unconscious, not those who study memory phenomena. It is conceivable though that the latter group could redefine the unconscious in terms of a multilayered memory system with short-term and long-term memory corresponding to preconscious and unconscious.

Memory and the unconscious may be intimately related, but to clearly distinguish the two is important for clarity. It is the contention of this book, in this section, to state that the construct of the unconscious and memory are sometimes confused. In other words, the construct of the unconscious is sometimes used to describe or explain events that really have to do with memory functionings. In fact, in the literature that does confuse the two constructs, one could substitute the word "memory" every place the author used the expression "the unconscious," and not suffer any loss of meaning. To paraphrase a popular expression "if it looks, sounds, and behaves like memory, it probably is memory." In such cases it should be called memory, and we should not import or conjure up some ambiguous construct such as the unconscious.

In the literature, there have been cases where the author used the words "subconscious" or "unconscious" (noun forms), but seemed to be really writing about memory events. Some examples of this include: 1) Morton Prince's *The Unconscious,* which is based entirely on his theory of "engrams"; 2) K. Koffka, who, in writing about the structure of the unconscious, was really writing about the structure of memory;[18] and 3) Gert Heilbrunn, who, in speculating about the unconscious, was dealing with the places in the brain where memories are stored and could be released by electrical stimulation.[19] Also, so much of many types of psychotherapy involves the recall and working with memories. The psychotherapist and patient search for earlier and earlier memories, looking for the core or nuclear memories. Many of the royal roads to the unconscious are really methods and techniques of memory retrieval. When it is a case of working with memories, there is no need to mystify the situation by speaking in terms of the unconscious.

W. H. R. Rivers once tried to distinguish the unconscious and memory. He argued that those experiences which cannot be brought into consciousness by any of the ordinary processes of memory or association be considered the contents of the unconscious. They can only be recalled by special conditions or techniques, such as, sleep, hypnotism, free association, and certain psychic states.[20] It is true that certain experiences require special techniques or conditions in order to be recalled, but that does not preclude the possibility that "ordinary processes of memory" are involved. There are motivational factors that allow some things to be recalled easily and others with great difficulty. The difference is in the difficulty involved not in the processes involved or in the place where the memory is stored.

We cannot say that memory phenomena can account for everything that happens in psychotherapy or that it can explain better everything that is sometimes talked about in terms of the unconscious. For example, memory processes alone cannot account for the way certain memories constellate themselves within the psychic system and sometimes behave as if they were autonomous complexes expressing intentionality. We are saying though that when the shoe of memory fits, it should be worn, and that we should not force the shoe of the unconscious on. To speak in terms of memory is a relatively more parsimonious way of speaking. We say relatively because we still do not know enough about memory and its operations. For example, we still do not know exactly how memories are recorded and retrieved. There are many theories about this but no conclusive ones. It is not our task to speculate on this but only to distinguish the unconscious and memory so that one source of confusion is removed.

## BIOFEEDBACK

Biofeedback is understood here as that endeavor to monitor and regulate autonomic activity within an individual, and sometimes by the individual himself. Biofeedback is considered in this book because the construct of the unconscious sometimes appears in biofeedback literature. Usually though, when the word "unconscious" is used, it appears in the expression "unconscious processes" and is synonymous with autonomic activities. Biofeedback is said to help us control unconscious processes. These processes include such autonomic activities as muscle tension, heartbeat, bloodflow, respiration, gland secretion, body temperature, and even some brain processes. The use of the word "unconscious" in relation to these activities is strictly descriptive (adjectival or adverbial), and the substitution of "autonomic" and/or "involuntary" for the word "unconscious" could be easily done without any loss of meaning. In fact, the former two expressions would be more descriptive.

Sometimes it is said that biofeedback can help us gain access to unconscious material in a sense different than just mentioned. The material in this case is not necessarily autonomic activities but refers to images, memories, and feelings. Here biofeedback is treated as another royal road to the unconscious. For example, David Danskin suggested that,

> Lowering EMG could result in increased production of primary process material and free association, learned and forgotten information, etc. . . . also, by increasing alpha and theta brain waves, one can achieve a state of reverie. While in this state, subjects often experience vivid hypnagogiclike images that they learn to bring to conscious awareness and describe, thus gaining new insights about themselves. The combination of alpha and theta feedback seems to facilitate extending self-awareness over normally unconscious processes.[21]

We see from Danskin's comments that biofeedback, like hypnotism and free association, can be a facilitator of the recovery of forgotten memories and of the conditions that allow other thought forms and activities to take place.

The underlying assumption that makes it possible to conceive of biofeedback as another road to the unconscious is that the person is a unity of mind and body. The corollary of this is that psychic events have physical corresponding events and vice versa. To conclude that a principle of strict causality is operating in either direction is unwarranted, but it is obvious that some kind of relationship exists between the psychic and the physical. What we have said up to this point poses no problem for the topic of the unconscious.

The problems begin when it is claimed that biofeedback can put us in contact with the unconscious. This leap, from looking at and interpreting the autonomic responses of the body and the psychic events that may attend these, to the conclusion of a thing called the unconscious is unwarranted and unnecessary unless one wanted to purposely mystify the situation. We will consider an example of this type of confusion.

Barbara Brown's book, *New Mind, New Body,* is a good introduction to biofeedback, but probably one of the most chaotic piece of writing regarding the construct of the unconscious. She did an excellent job in presenting the principles, methods, and equipment of biofeedback. She did a very poor job, though, when she tried to account for the phenomena in terms of the unconscious. She referred to the expression "subconscious" most of the time, but also used the expressions "unconscious," "nonconscious," and "subliminal" as if they were synonymous. She never defined or distinguished these terms. She used the word "subconscious" as a noun, an adjective, and as an adverb. Sometimes she used it to imply a thing and sometimes to imply a place. Further, she used expressions, such as, "inner physical self," and the "skin's mind."

Brown made the leap from the observation and measuring of auto-nomic responses to the conclusion of a thing called "the sub-conscious" responsible for such responses. A blatant example of this is revealed by her title for chapter three "Skin talk: Conversations with the Subconscious." We said earlier that psychic states have corre-sponding physical expressions; for example, anxiety can increase skin secretion, and, by observing the latter, we can reasonably conclude the former. We cannot, though, reasonably conclude that a skin response is caused by something referred to as "the subconscious." The epitome of Brown's theoretical extravagance is this definition she gave of biofeedback: "The self teaching the self to control the inner self."[22] This multiplication of selves is unwarranted and unnecessary given what she is looking at, that is, autonomic responses.

The confusion exemplified by Barbara Brown is the exception and not the rule regarding literature dealing with biofeedback. When the word "unconscious" does appear, it is used descriptively and clearly referring to autonomic activities. It is contended here that, by keep-ing the problematic noun form of the word "unconscious" out of this type of literature, one more source of confusion surrounding the construct of the unconscious will be removed.

## AUTOMATIC BEHAVIOR

In 1846 Carl Gustav Carus wrote that living was a process of making unconscious what is conscious. In our century, Sigmund Freud argued that it was important to make conscious that which is unconscious. It seems that the two men were contradicting one another. This would be true if both men were referring to the same thing when they used the words "conscious" and "unconscious." They were not. Freud was referring to something that occurs during psychotherapy where unconscious memories, feelings, and conflicts are induced to become conscious so that they can be worked out. Without this happening, there is no psychotherapy and no cure. Carus was alluding to something that happens every day and to everyone, that is, the experience of learning a skill or acquiring a habit. We all know how it is to learn to ride a bicycle, learn the techniques of a new sport, the manual skills of a trade or a musical instrument, or simply how to acquire any habit. In the beginning the process is difficult, awkward, unevenly executed, full of effort and concentration, and slow-going. After practicing and repeating the behavior over and over, we can perform the activity without effort, without thinking about it, automatically. We also know that unless something does become automatic, it is not usually performed well. This is common knowledge to every musician, sportsman, and manually skilled worker.

What we have just described is what is referred to as "automatic behavior" (or automatism). As we said, this is an everyday occurring and observable event. The problem, regarding our topic, begins when we try to account for these events in terms of the unconscious. There usually is no problem in referring to automatic behavior as unconscious behavior or behavior performed unconsciously, but there are problems when automatic behavior is said to be performed by the unconscious. What we have here is another case, like that discussed regarding biofeedback, of a leap from observable behavior to an entity responsible for that behavior. Calling that entity "the unconscious" only serves to mystify the situation, not clarify or explain it. We will examine some examples of the overlapping of the construct of the unconscious with the phenomenon of automatic behavior.

Automatic behavior is sometimes appealed to as a proof for the unconscious or unconscious mental states. In fact, William James, in considering ten so-called proofs for unconscious mental states, discussed automatic behavior as one of those proofs and concluded that it was not. He contended that the behavior in question is not necessarily unconscious, but that it could be performed so fast and inattentively that no memory of the process remains. Also, he suggested that it could be performed by split-off cortical consciousness.[23] James was opting for the more parsimonious accounting of the phenomenon.

Leopold Bellak, in discussing the unconscious, distinguished two types—physiological unconscious and configurational unconscious. The former relates to "the unawareness of most vegetative and neurological processes in the individual," the latter relates to the unawareness involved in how we come to learn skills which become automatic.[24] The distinction between the two types of unawareness's is significant, but calling them two different unconsciouses is not necessary and only adds to the stockpile of neologisms. Leaving it as two types of unawarenesses would have been more descriptive and less mystifying.

In reference to Russian psychology, R. Bassin and A. Sherozia made the point that there is one school of thought that would prefer to understand the unconscious only as automatism.[25] Here we have an extreme case of a restricted interpretation of what is referred to by the unconscious.

In the popular literature, W. Timothy Gallwey's *The Inner Game of Tennis* is based predominantly on the principles and phenomena of automatism. Rather than deal with the topic on that level, Gallwey embellished his book with allusions to an unconscious mind that is distinct from the self-conscious mind. The former, which at various times he referred to as "servant," "computer," "memory bank," "Self 2," and "He," is based in the spinal and midbrain areas of the nervous system. "It" is the better tennis player of the two minds. One has only to learn how to let "It" learn and perform the techniques of tennis.[26] Gallwey's advice regarding tennis is very good, and to the extent that he based his ideas on automatism they are sound; but his theoretical embellishments are unnecessary, confusing, and mystifying.

We have seen from the preceding examples that the construct of the unconscious has been related to the phenomena of automatic behaviors. It is contended that such association is a confusion of two things. Admittedly we do not know exactly how to account for automatic behavior. Until we have such knowledge, it is argued that the more parsimonious accounting of the phenomenon be promoted and not explained in terms of some unconscious.

Knowledge of the speed and ability of the brain has a bearing on the understanding of automatic behavior. As yet, we do not have enough knowledge about this matter. We have some sense of the speed of processing information from our experience with computers, but we do not yet have a sense of just how fast our brains can process information. There is no need to posit that some unconscious is responsible for certain behaviors. It is possible that the brain can carry out more than one thought process at a time, or that it could alternate rapidly between two or more processes. Most of us can drive a car, carry on a conversation, listen to the radio, and stay on the road. We may feel that these activities are happening simultaneously, but it is also possible that our brain is rapidly alternating its attention between these activities. Certainly, we would not say that different minds are performing each function. Until we have an adequate appraisal of the brain's abilities, it is suggested that automatic behavior and the unconscious be clearly distinguished. With such a distinction, another source of confusion will be removed.

## SUBLIMINAL PERCEPTION

The construct of the unconscious has been associated with the phenomenon of subliminal perception in two ways. In one way, the word "subconscious" (as opposed to "unconscious"), as an adjective or adverb, is the most common expression used. In the second way, both expressions—"unconscious" and "subconscious," in the noun form—have been used. We will see that the latter practice is the problematic one.

The expressions "unconscious perception," "subconscious perception," and "subliminal perception" are virtually synonymous. They usually refer to perception below a certain threshold of awareness. Of the three adjectives, subliminal is the most descriptive one because it translates most closely into the meaning intended. Also, one avoids the problem of defining what conscious means. It is easier to define and agree upon threshold levels than to agree on a definition of consciousness. We recommend that, when subthreshold events are referred to, the term "subliminal" be used and the terms "sub- or unconscious" be avoided. For the most part this is the practice used by writers on the subject of subliminal perception, so there is relatively little problem here regarding the topic of the unconscious.

The problems begin when subliminal events are spoken of in terms of the unconscious. The implication here is that subliminal perception is a function of the unconscious. In other words, a person contains an unconscious which perceives and responds to stimuli without the person's immediate, direct awareness of what is happening. Here again we have a case, like that discussed in regard to biofeedback and automatic behavior, of a theoretical leap from the event of subliminal perception to the conclusion of an entity responsible for such an event. Such leaps are unwarranted because we do not know enough about the capabilities people are endowed with. The conjuring up of an entity such as the unconscious that resides in a person and is responsible for certain behavior is arbitrary, unnecessary, and mystifying. It is one thing to state that people are able to perceive stimuli below the normal level of awareness, but quite another thing to contend that the unconscious in the persons is perceiving. The former statement is almost universally accepted, the latter one is unacceptable to most investigators in this field (subliminal perception).

It must be emphasized here that this practice of alluding to an entity is the exception and not the rule in the literature on subliminal phenomena. Physiological psychologists usually avoid entirely the construct of the unconscious. It is some of those who speculate upon the work of physiologists who can cause the theoretical confusion regarding the topic. A good example of this is Virginia Adams' account of Lloyd Silverman's work.

In 1975, Silverman published an account of his experiments with what he referred to as "subliminal psychodynamic activation."[27] Essentially what he did was to flash, with a tachistoscope, such messages as "Mommy and I are one," or "Beating daddy is O.K.," and observe the differential effect on manifest psychopathology. In that article, he never used the noun form of the word "unconscious," but only used the adjectival form. His work is highly suggestive, but not conclusive. Recently Virginia Adams gave an accounting of Silverman's work but used the noun form of the word "unconscious" implying a place or a thing and that Silverman had managed to reach the unconscious with his subliminal messages. The title used for the article—"'Mommy and I Are One,' Beaming Messages to Inner Space"—suggested as much. [29] Such expressions may be creative but they are misleading regarding the construct of the unconscious.

Literary practice of the type displayed by Adams is the exception and not the rule in the reporting on subliminal studies. In this book, we want to identify this potential source of confusion and recommend that it be guarded against, especially because the question of subliminal perception is still an unsettled one. There are many variables that enter into the process of perception, such as stimuli, state, and motivational factors. This has given rise to many debates about methods, controls, and criteria. Because of these conditions, any statement about subliminal perception is usually a qualified one.

There is much about subliminal perception that we still do not know. Most would agree that some degree of subliminal perception goes on. It can be demonstrated that a subject will discriminate and respond to subliminal stimuli without being able to report about it. This can easily lead to the conclusion that something or some process in the subject registered the stimuli in order to react to it. But the question of how the subject actually perceives subliminally is still unanswered. The theories are still debated and there is a wide range of them. From the bio-physical standpoint, some argue that it is a function of neurons only, or that it is a right-brain activity. From the transpersonal-spiritual standpoint, it is argued that subliminal perception is a function of the soul or the unconscious. Some say that a person has spiritual senses that correspond to his physical senses. Given the lack of knowledge in this area, it is understandable how a construct of the unconscious can be used to fill in the gap in our knowledge. Even so, there are more parsimonious explanations to consider before we postulate that some thing is involved. Subliminal perception may be a variation of normal perception which, in turn, is one of the many abilities of a human being. There is no need to assign certain, as yet unexplanable, actions to some mysterious entity within the human being.

One last point to consider is related to the work and speculations of Howard Shevrin and Scott Dickman. They suggested that the assumption of a psychological unconscious was a necessary assumption for all psychological theories.[29] They based this claim on their work with subliminal events. What they meant by psychological unconscious refers to that class of psychological events that are at the time unknown to the subject but that actively influence the subject's behavior. The psychological events that they were talking about have to do with complex perceptual discriminations, thinking in the form of associations, selection, and decisions made *without* the benefit of consciousness. This, in turn, was based on findings from selective attention studies, subliminal perception studies, and certain visual phenomena involving perceptual processing.

They offered their findings as a way to close the gap between the lab and the clinic, with its psychoanalytic definition of the unconscious. If psychological functions could be shown to go on without awareness, then that is the essential point required by the psychoanalytic assumption of a psychological unconscious.

Shevrin's and Dickman's work is a forward step toward the rapproachment of the lab and the clinic, but the opening question and title of their article is misleading. They asked if the assumption of a psychological unconscious was necessary for psychological theories. They then proceeded to show that some psychological processes can go on without consciousness. The answer to their question is yes, it is necessary for theories to accept that unconscious psychological processes go on; but, no, those theories need not be articulated in terms of a psychological unconscious. The shift from the adjectival usage of the word "unconscious" to the noun form may appear insignificant but there is a great difference in the implications attached to the two usages. It is precisely being aware of this distinction that makes the difference between a construct of the unconscious and subliminal phenomena being confused or not.

## CONDITIONING

In discussing conditioning, we will consider the classical model, with the interoceptive model as a variation of it, and also the operant conditioning model. The study of conditioning falls within the purview of experimental psychology. Experimental psychology represents one of the major challengers of the construct of the unconscious. As a matter of fact, experimental psychologists will usually have nothing to do with any mentalistic constructs such as mind, conscious, self, unconscious, personality, and so forth. As can be expected, representatives of this school of thought prefer to define the unconscious, if at all, in terms of either behavioral manifestations, physiological mechanisms, or operational definitions. In short, the construct of the unconscious is usually not associated with conditioning; in fact, the former is clearly reduced to the latter, and hence there is no confusion in the literature dealing with conditioning regarding the construct of the unconscious. We discuss conditioning here, though, because the principles, manner, and phenomena of conditioning are sometimes helpful in accounting for certain behaviors otherwise explained in terms of some unconscious.

Ivan Pavlov's conditioned-reflex model involves forming a conditioned response to some external stimulus such as a bell, or a light. Pavlov also enunciated the principle that any variation of the *internal* environment of an animal which is associated with an unconditioned activity, may become a conditioned reflex, that is, a means of knowing the environment and shaping behavior.[30] This principle is the foundation of what has come to be known as interoceptive conditioning.

Interoceptive conditioning is classical conditioning in which the conditioned stimulus or the unconditioned stimulus or both are delivered to mucous membrane of some specific internal organ. As E. Airapetyantz and K. Bykov wrote,

> [One] stimulus acts only on their (dogs) internal organ under conditions which completely exclude the possibility of simultaneous stimulation of the exteroceptors. Simultaneously another stimulus is applied which evokes some unconditioned reflex. It is clear that if the stimulus which acts on the internal organ calls forth a conditioned reflex, this shows, first, that interoceptors exist within the given internal organ, and, second, that the impulses from the interoceptors can reach the brain, resulting in the formation of a temporary connection.[31]

Interoceptive conditioning has been conducted with animal and human subjects.[32] In both cases it is demonstrated that impulses from internal organs do reach the brain, that they can be considered subliminal, and can become signals for higher neural activities.

Airapetyantz and Bykov argued that, for them, interoceptive phenomena accounted adequately for what is usually assigned to the unconscious (they used the word "subconscious"). We do not have to agree wholeheartedly with them, but they do show us something significant about human behavior, that is, that conditioning can go on not only in relation to external stimuli but also with internal ones.

The experimentation and the technology of interoceptive conditioning is modern, but the idea of it is old. The notion that subtle, obscure sensations that arise from within the organism and influence its behavior and mood has been written about before. For example, in 1771 a physiologist named J. A. Unzer wrote about what he referred to as "unconscious thinking," which had to do precisely with those subtle internal sensations.[33] In 1846, Carl Carus coined the expression "sentience" to distinguish those subtle internal sensations from sensations arising from the external environment. Carus believed that the internal sensations were related to the human soul.[34] It may be that our interoceptive conditioning experimentors have uncovered the basic mechanism involved in what Unzer and Carus have alluded to but without calling it either unconscious thinking or a soul function.

The final conditioning model that will be considered is the operant conditioning one developed by B. F. Skinner. Skinner considered constructs such as self, unconscious, personality, and so forth as convenient, shorthand, hypothetical expressions used by some to help explain to themselves and others why people do what they do. He considered the construct of the unconscious as one we use to fill in the gap in our knowledge of some cause. Skinner accused Freud of following the traditional pattern of looking for a cause of human behavior inside the organism.[35] Skinner would not accept any talk about entities, and according to him the concepts of self, unconscious or conscious, are not essential in an analysis of behavior. Whereas Freud treated behavior as merely the symptom of a neurosis, Skinner would make behavior the beginning, essence, and end of therapy. Skinner contended that, in fact, *patterns of behavior* survive through the years, not aggression, guilt, etc.[36]

Skinner rewrote the story of the defense mechanisms. Regarding such mechanisms as repression, reaction-formation, rationalization, sublimation, fantasy, dreams, displacement, wit, identification, projection, slips, forgetting, self-punishment, and physical symptoms, Skinner wrote,

> Such manifestations are simply the responses of a person who has had a particular history. They are neither symptoms nor the surreptitious expression of repressed wishes or impulses . . . pent-up emotion is not the cause of disordered behavior, it is part of it. Not being able to recall an early memory does not produce neurotic symptoms; it is itself an example of ineffective behavior. It is quite possible that in therapy the pent-up emotion and the behavioral symptom may disappear at the same time or that a repressed memory will be recalled when maladjusted behavior has been corrected. But this does not mean that one of these events is the cause of the other. They may both have been products of an environmental history which therapy has altered.[37]

The core principle with which Skinner operated was expressed one time in this way,

> Behavior which is so troublesome or dangerous as to be said to characterize mental disease may also simply be learned—that is, it may be the product of reinforcing contingencies which effect the organism according to learning processes encountered in the behavior of the normal individual.[38]

Skinner would not entertain metaphysical, metaphorical, and mystifying notions. He did not look for the mysterious and tried not to create any. Given a phenomenon to analyze, he would investigate the history of reinforcement and punishment involved, and look for any other variables that may have *shaped* a particular behavior. He believed that what a person manifests as behavior is simply *learned* and not the result of the obscure workings of some inner force or entity.

What has been learned intentionally or haphazardly can be un-learned. This, in short, is Skinner's principle and program for diagnosis and psychotherapy.

We have heard from the experimental psychologists. They have revealed some important insights about the factors that can and do influence human behavior in very subtle ways. The construct of the unconscious has no meaning for these psychologists except as it is reinterpreted in terms of the unawareness associated with one or more of the conditioning models that we have presented. They feel confident that they can account for phenomena sometimes attributed to the unconscious by referring to the various principles of learning theory.

## CONCLUSION

In looking back over the material that was presented within the Bio-Physical Approach, some summary and concluding comments can be made.

1) Representatives of this approach are committed to investigate and interpret behavior, phenomena, and events solely in terms of bio-physical factors. Regarding the construct of the unconscious, they are disposed to understand, define, and reduce it in terms of some measurable variables.

2) We have been concerned to identify and remove sources of confusion within this approach. Sometimes the construct of the unconscious is employed to account for behavior that could be more descriptively and parsimoniously explained in terms of one or more of the following: memory processes, automatic behavior, physiological mechanisms, subliminal perception, and conditioning. When there is confusion regarding these things, it is said that the unconscious is responsible for these activities. In such cases, the unconscious functions like an X-factor that is not explained but only presumed to account for the cause of some behavior. As such, the expression "the unconscious" tells us very little, tends to mystify the situation, and is not really necessary. We said that this represented an unwarranted theoretical leap from observed behavior to the positing of an entity

responsible for the behavior. It does the topic of the unconscious a disservice to be confused in this manner. It should be stressed that it is the noun form of the word "unconscious" that is problematic in the Bio-Physical Approach. This noun-form usage does not belong in that approach, is superfluous, and should be avoided in order to prevent certain types of confusion regarding the construct of the unconscious.

3) Regarding the overall program of a typological investigation of the construct of the unconscious, the Bio-Physical Approach serves well as a devil's advocate vis-à-vis the other three approaches. The Bio-Physical Approach is a good place to begin any analysis of phenomena and behavior. It provides a checklist. When faced with some behavior to account for, we should first eliminate the possibility or evaluate the degree of the behavior being accounted for in terms of bio-physical activities such as automatic behavior, conditioning, subliminal events, and so forth, before we begin to entertain other explanatory theories. We say "should" because we are advocating the principle of parsimony. We want to prevent the creation and the use of pseudo-explanatory entities and want nothing to be assumed as a necessary explanation unless it is established by evident experience or scientific testing.

The successive chapters will deal with other theories of human behavior centered on a construct of the unconscious but not primarily grounded in a bio-physical approach. These other theories do not necessarily exclude consideration of the bio-physical components of behavior, but they do not heavily emphasize them or focus almost exclusively on them. In general, the theorists dealt with in the subsequent three approaches tend to view the bio-physical factors as having a limited value in explaining human behavior. For example, in the next approach the theorists prefer to speak in terms of ideas, feelings, and so forth. It is the value of any genuine typological inquiry to let all points of view be represented and to prevent any one approach from monopolizing the topic area with its own parochial methods and vocabulary.

The construct of the unconscious has been employed for the most part to answer the question "why?" The matrix of causes surrounding any one act is more complex than any one approach can adequately account for. We have just considered one set of factors that center on a bio-physical approach toward the understanding of behavior.

# Notes

1. See pages 7–10 to match these expressions with the theorist who used them. We will present such lists in the beginning of each approach.

2. Gert Heilbrunn, "Biologic Correlates of Psychoanalytic Concepts," *Journal of American Psychoanalytic Association* 27, no. 3 (1979), p. 597.

3. Justin Neuman, "The Existence of the Freudian Unconscious in the Structure and Functions of the Nervous System," *Psychoanalytic Review* 36 (1949), pp. 355–64.

4. William Calwell, "The Unconscious: A Suggestion," *The Journal of Medical Science* LXXI (1952), pp. 97–100.

5. Gert Heilbrunn, "The Neurobiologic Aspect of Three Psychoanalytic Concepts," *Comprehensive Psychiatry* 5, no. 5 (1961), pp. 261–68.

6. Geoffrey Osler, "The Changing Image of Human Nature: The Biological Aspect," *American Journal of Psychoanalysis* 26–27 (1966–67), pp. 130–38.

7. Conrad Chyatte et al., "Brain Blood-Shift Theory: Verification of a Predicted Gradient in Tactual-Auditory Rivalry," *International Journal of Neuropsychiatry* 3–4, no. 1 (1967–68), pp. 360–64.

8. Sally Springer and Georg Deutsch, *Left Brain, Right Brain* (San Francisco, California: W. H. Freeman and Co., 1981), pp. 197–99.

9. Eduard von Hartmann, *The Philosophy of the Unconscious* (London: Routledge & Kegan Paul, 1950), p. 270.

10. Springer and Deutsch, *Left Brain, Right Brain,* p. 199.

11. David Galin, "Implications for Psychiatry of Left and Right Cerebral Specialization," *Archives of General Psychiatry* 31 (October 1974), p. 572.

12. Rhawn Joseph, "Awareness, The Origin of Thought, and the Role of Conscious Self-Deception in Resistance and Repression," *Psychological Reports* 46 (1980), p. 779.

13. We could also include here T. Blakeslee, who in his book *The Right Brain* (A new understanding of the unconscious mind and its creative powers), acknowledged his debt to Galin, and considered the right hemisphere as the "unconscious mind."

14. Springer and Deutsch, *Left Brain, Right Brain,* p. 101.

15. Ibid., p. 219.

16. Henri Ellenberger, "The Unconscious Before Freud," *Bulletin of the Menninger Clinic* 21, no. 3 (1957), pp. 3–15. Also, see Morton Prince's *The Unconscious* concerning engrams.

17. T. Bilikiewicz, "Total Somatechomy and Its Psychopathological Consequences," *Polish Medical Journal* 8, no. 2 (1969), pp. 490–91.

18. K. Koffka, "On the Structure of the Unconscious," in *The Unconscious, A Symposium*, ed., C. M. Child (New York: Alfred A. Knopf, 1927), pp. 43–68.

19. Gert Heilbrunn, "The Neurobiologic Aspect of Three Psychoanalytic Concepts," *Comprehensive Psychiatry* 2, no. 5 (1961), pp. 261–68.

20. W. H. R. Rivers, *Instinct and the Unconscious* (London: Cambridge University Press, 1924), p. 9.

21. David Danskin and E. Dale Walter, "Biofeedback and Voluntary Self-Regulation: Counseling and Education," *Personal and Guidance Journal* 51, no. 9 (1973), p. 636.

22. Barbara Brown, *New Mind, New Body* (New York: Bantam Books, 1974), p. 18. We can add here that in the popular literature another variation of this type of confusion is exemplified by Julius Fast's book *Body Language*. His careless use of the noun form of the word "unconscious" gives the impression that he is referring to an entity. He endows the physical body, via this mysterious unconscious, with independent, telegraphing power. He is ultimately dealing with body behavior, either involuntarily controlled like the widening of the pupils when the person sees something pleasant, or voluntarily controlled like crossing one's legs or arms to indicate resistance.

23. William James, *The Principles of Psychology* (New York: H. Holt & Co., 1893), pp. 164ff.

24. Leopold Bellak, "The Unconscious," *Annals of the New York Academy of Sciences* 76 (1959), pp. 1070–71.

25. F. V. Bassin and A. E. Sherozia, "The Role of the Category of the Unconscious in the System of the Present-Day Scientific Knowledge of the Mind," paper presented at the International Symposium on the Problem of the Unconscious, Tbilisi, USSR, 1979, p. 9.

26. W. Timothy Gallwey, *The Inner Game of Tennis* (New York: Bantam Books, 1974).

27. Lloyd Silverman, "An Experimental Method for the Study of Unconscious Conflict," *British Journal of Medical Psychology* 48 (1975), pp. 291–98.

28. Virginia Adams, " 'Mommy and I are One,' Beaming Messages to Inner Space," *Psychology Today* (May, 1982), pp. 24–36.

29. Howard Shevrin and Scott Dickman, "The Psychological Unconscious, A Necessary Assumption for all Psychological Theory?" *American Psychologist* (May 1980), pp. 421–33.

30. E. Airapetyantz and K. Bykov, "Physiological Experiments and the Psychology of the Subconscious," *Philosophy and Phenomenological Research* 5 (1945), p. 581.

31. Ibid., p. 584.

32. A good reference for this is G. Razan, "The Observable Unconscious and the Inferable Conscious in Current Soviet Psychophysiology," *Psychological Review* 68 (1961), pp. 81–147. The title of this article is curious and misleading. Razran is dealing strictly with interoceptive conditioning, and refers to it as the "the observable unconscious." What he means by "observable" is that he can measure the stimulus and response strength. There should be no confusion here that he is

referring to any other understanding of "the unconscious" except in his own restricted way—having to do with interceptive phenomena.

33. M. Altschule, "The Growth of the Concept of Unconscious Cerebration Before 1890," in *Roots of Modern Psychiatry* (New York: Grune & Stratton, 1965), p. 60.

34. Carl G. Carus, *Psyche* (New York: Spring Publications, 1970), pp. 37ff.

35. B. F. Skinner, "A Critique of Psychoanalytic Concepts and Ideas," in *Cumulative Record* (New York: Appleton-Century-Crofts, Inc., 1959), p. 187.

36. Ibid., p. 191.

37. B. F. Skinner, *Science and Human Behavior* (New York: Macmillan Co., 1953), pp. 378–79.

38. Skinner, *Cumulative Record,* p. 199.

# Chapter III

# Psycho-Personal Approach

## Introduction

"Psycho-Personal" is the second major generic term of this typological study. It represents that aggregate of literature that discusses the unconscious as a function of psychological factors and as related to an individual's personal history.

In this section of the book, we move from the realm of the experimental lab to the setting of the clinic and the psychotherapeutic chair. We shift from the world of tests, measurements, and experiments to the world of listening, talking, and interpreting. The medium of exchange is words not numbers.

The neologisms that have appeared within this framework include:

| | |
|---|---|
| Deep Psychological Unconscious | Psychological Unconscious |
| Apperceptive Unconscious | Psychodynamic Unconscious |
| Emotional Unconscious | Personal Unconscious |
| Relative Unconscious | Latent Self |
| Rational Unconscious | Dynamic Unconscious |
| Preconscious | Acquired Unconscious |
| Subconscious | Freudian Unconscious |
| Unconscious | Submerged Unconscious |
| Dreaming Mind | Familiar Unconscious |
| Cognitive Unconscious | Embedded Unconscious |
| Id | Familial Unconscious |

This multiplication of neologisms only impedes the progress of the understanding of the subject matter, especially because many of the above are really synonymous expressions.

In the literature considered in this approach the word "unconscious" appears as a noun, an adjective, and as an adverb. The latter two forms are usually not problematic. The problems arise from the noun form usage of the word. In the noun form, one can easily get the impression that the expression "the unconscious" is referring to some thing existing within a person and working behind the scenes of that person's life. Those writers who do employ the noun form sometimes issue warnings precisely not to imply that a substantive entity is involved. For the reader, though, it is hard to remember these warnings when one reads sentence after sentence wherein the noun form is used, and the suggestion is that the author is referring to a subsistent entity. For example, Sigmund Freud and Carl Jung both cautioned against reification of the construct of the unconscious, but these two theorists are most responsible for giving the impression that the unconscious refers to an entity.

We will begin this chapter by first presenting the ideas of those who made extensive use of the noun form of the word "unconscious," which implied that an autonomous, active agent is involved. Then we will consider other theorists who did not use the noun form of the word and who, in fact, objected to such practice. Instead, these other theorists preferred to analyze and reinterpret the behavior in question without using the expression "the unconscious." Some have reacted strongly against those who reified the construct. Ironically, although most people presented in this approach objected to the use of the noun form, of the three who did use it, two (Freud and Jung) dominate the subject area over all other points of view combined in terms of the literary output centered on their system of ideas. This is not to say that Freud or Jung necessarily had the right point of view, but only to make a statement about the state of the literature on the topic of the unconscious to this point.

## The Repressed Unconscious

The best-known example of a psycho-personal type of understanding of the unconscious is that which sees it as a function of repressed material. Suppressed material could also be included here. "The repressed" refers to the sum of material, such as, memories, impulses, feelings, experiences, perceptions, wishes, ideas, and so forth, that is kept from conscious awareness because of its unacceptable and/or painful nature. We say "is kept" because supposedly something in us keeps this material from our consciousness without our awareness of its happening. *It happens* unconsciously. "The suppressed" refers to all that was just said, except that with suppression we have some awareness of what is happening. *We do it* consciously. Sigmund Freud, the chief exponent of this point of view, postulated something he called a "censor" that did the work of repression. The work of suppression is done by the ego. The problems posed by this formulation will be discussed in a subsequent section. For now, we will let this formulation stand and present those theorists who developed this line of argument. These include Sigmund Freud, Carl Jung, and Otto Rank. These are the three alluded to in the introduction who used the noun form of the word "unconscious."

Referring back to our list of neologisms, it can be said that many of them relate to this understanding of what the unconscious refers to.

## SIGMUND FREUD

Where does one begin to talk about Sigmund Freud when one considers all the books, articles, dissertations, and papers that have been written about him and his ideas? The Freudian slip is virtually a household word. In this century, he is directly and indirectly responsible for most of the literature on the topic of the unconscious. Right or wrong, he is the central figure in this area. It is rare to read anything regarding the unconscious without encountering a reference to Freud.

We will continue these introductory remarks by considering two comments, which convey another dimension of the impact of Freud. S. David House in 1928 wrote,

> We may get a bird's-eye view of the intellectual distance theorizing has traveled for good or ill since 1600 by juxtaposing the Cartesian dictum,

"I think, therefore I am" and the Freudian dictum, "I desire, therefore I think."[1]

In 1979, Mario Rendon wrote,

Freud has turned Descartes' famous and long-standing "I think, therefore I exist" into something like "I think from where I do not even think I exist."[2]

These imaginative sentences dramatize the shift in focus and emphasis that Freud induced with his ideas about the unconscious.

It has been said that Descartes, by strictly identifying the mental with the conscious, created the problem of the unconscious. The problem had been expressed in the question of whether or not unconscious mental states exist. In 1893, William James concluded that they do not. A little later, Freud took up the question and believed that he had finally put the matter to rest by proving that unconscious mental states must exist. When James wrote, Freud's ideas were not published, but from James' discussion of the third proof in favor of unconscious mental states we can derive a model to help understand Freud's posture regarding the unconscious.

In the so-called third proof, James referred to that experience in which, for example, one thinks of A, and C comes to mind. B is the natural logical link, but we have no awareness of B. Some have concluded that B exists in an unconscious state. This was considered by some to be a proof of the unconscious. James, though, would rather believe that B was there in consciousness, but was quickly forgotten or that B's "brain tract" alone was adequate to link A to C.

If we drop James' specific reference, this ABC model is an excellent paradigm of the Freudian enterprise. Much of Freud's methodology can be understood with this model, that is, fill in all gaps between any A and C with B. B was to be found in the unconscious. Psychoanalysis, as a form of psychotherapy, is basically the process of uncovering all B's in a Sherlock Holmsian style of attending to seemingly insignificant clues in the attempt to deduce the "real" meaning of a particular symptom or behavior. What the B's are and how they got into the unconscious is the heart of Freud's theory of repression. This is a simplified model, but there is little in the Freudian literature that could not conform to this model. We can now introduce the theory of repression.

As a physician, Freud was constantly faced with patients who wanted help with their problems. Freud's challenge was to make sense of the patient's abnormal behavior. Many times the patient's explanation did not fit all the facts, or was inappropriate. Sometimes the symptom appeared meaningless. In short, both Freud and his patient were searching for an answer to the question "why?"

Freud proceeded on the strength of his conviction that everything could be explained because everything is determined. With this faith, he was relentless in his search for meaning. When the patient's explanation was not enough, Freud assumed and looked for the balance of the explanation in the unconscious of the patient. This led to his conviction that the mind was more than consciousness. This, plus his observations regarding hypnosis, dreams, slips, and forgotten childhood experiences, led him to posit the existence of the unconscious. The gain in meaning this hypothesis provided strengthened his faith in its legitimacy and necessity.

If we recall our ABC model, we can say that Freud knew where the missing B's were. They were in the unconscious. His method of free association and dream analysis allowed him to recover the missing B's. Now the question becomes "why are the B's missing?" The answer involves the phenomenon of repression.

In 1923, Freud wrote "thus we obtain our concept of the unconscious from the theory of repression."[3] Essentially, repression is the turning away and keeping the incompatible, unacceptable, and painful material from reaching consciousness. This can include unacceptable libidinal impulses, wishes, feelings, thought, and so forth, that would make one feel guilty or that which would bring on punishment, or anything that may result in the losing of the approval of our parents and friends. Freud made the comment that repressed material—for example, an intolerable wish—may be kept from the conscious, but that "it continues to exist in the unconscious . . . and . . . on the look-out for an opportunity of being activated."[4] Here we get a picture of the unconscious as, not only the place for the repressed, but also as a dynamic system, active in the pursuit of gratifying its wishes. The repressed wishes constantly exert influence on outward behavior and consequently require an equally constant counterforce to keep them in check.

The models that Freud developed to explain how repression worked underwent three major changes in his lifetime. Up to 1900, Freud made use a *neurological-economic model*. With this model he understood that mental events were a function of an entity called "psyche." This psyche needed energy to function. It derived its energy from libido. Libido referred to the energy of those instincts related to love. Libido was ultimately a function of the physical organs. These instincts were repressed as wishes that sought the discharge of energy. Freud found this model inadequate. Some have contended that Freud never really gave up this model but only substituted psychological words for the neurological ones. Freud's theory could be considered a theory of instincts and their vicissitudes.

In the year 1900, Freud introduced the *topographic model*. This model used the expressions "conscious," "unconscious," and "preconscious." The unconscious is made up of repressed wishes, drives, ideas, and memories. These were inadmissible to consciousness except through special methods. Preconscious material was admissible to consciousness without much difficulty. Between unconscious and preconscious and between the preconscious and the conscious operated what he called "censors" that determined what material would be admissible without causing undue conflict for consciousness. When Freud found more in the unconscious besides repressed material, he developed this next model.

In 1923, Freud presented his *structural model*. This model uses the expressions "id," "ego," and "superego." Where before the repressed was equal to the unconscious, he now found that not all that was unconscious was repressed. The word "id" covers this enlarged area of repressed and unrepressed unconscious elements. Freud came to realize that in the unconscious operated forces working against the satisfaction of the instinctual drives. There were the forces of repression.

These he identified as the unconscious aspects of the ego (including the superego and ego ideal).

With the development of this last model, Freud felt that he had adequately comprehended the contents of the unconscious.

It should be mentioned that Freud also referred to what he called "archaic heritages" as being part of the unconscious. These are part of the unrepressed unconscious and are related to those patterns or tendencies that we inherit from our ancestors. This aspect of his theory will be discussed in the Socio-Cultural Approach under the heading "racial unconscious."

We will encounter some of Freud's ideas again in the following sections in contrast or comparison with other ideas. Here we wanted to focus on this theory of repression. A useful way to summarize and present a more complete picture of the Freudian unconscious is this sentence by Ellenberger:

> This unconscious of the repressed is the seat of active, primitive, brutish, infantile, aggressive, and sexual drives; it follows exclusively the principle of pleasure, ignores time, death, logic, values, and morals; it manifests itself through dreams, symbols, parapraxis, symptomatic actions, and neurotic symptoms.[5]

## CARL G. JUNG

Carl Jung had an appreciation of the unconscious that spans the four major types presented in this book. In other words, he wrote about the unconscious at various times in such a way that revealed his appreciation of the bio-physical, psycho-personal, socio-cultural, and transpersonal-spiritual dimensions of it. Precisely because of his unique breadth of understanding, Jung's idea will be presented in several places. He is given special attention in three out of the four approaches of this typology.[6] Next to Freud, Jung is the other prominent figure on the topic of the unconscious. These two are usually mentioned in tandem whenever the subject is presented.

Among the reasons why Jung eventually broke away from Freud was their difference of opinion on the nature of the unconscious.

Although they both recognized the connection between the repressed and the unconscious, each assigned a different place and value to repressed material. Whereas Freud built his theory on the phenomenon of repression, Jung gave repressed material only a limited position in his theory.

According to Jung, the realm of the repressed is only one sector of the unconscious. He thought that because Freud limited his understanding to only the repressed material, Freud would naturally depreciate the unconscious and give it a negative connotation. For Jung the unconscious was for the most part a positive aspect and was to be trusted. It was not to be replaced or controlled as Freud would have it. Jung also thought that Freud overestimated how much could be accounted for by reducing everything to only repressed libidinal impulses.

So far we have focused on differences. Freud's and Jung's ideas do overlap in one significant way. Everything Freud posited as contents of the unconscious, Jung assigned to what he called the "personal unconscious." In Jung's system, the phenomenon of repression related only to the realm of the personal unconscious. Jung himself commented on this overlapping with Freud's theory.[7] The only exception is that Jung located what Freud referred to as "archaic heritages" in what he (Jung) called the "collective unconscious."

The contents of the personal unconscious include: repressed experiences, forgotten material, subliminal perceptions, suppressed thoughts and feelings, material too feeble to enter consciousness, feeling-toned complexes, and anything else of a personal, acquired, and individual nature. The personal unconscious is only the beginning or the most superficial layer of the unconscious. Jung claimed to have found more and to have gone deeper into the unconscious, into what he referred to as "the collective unconscious." He came to this hypothesis because, in analysis, he found that he could not make sense of all the patient's unconscious by only considering the personal experiences of the patient. In fact, Jung contended that sometimes interpretations based only on personal history were not enough and that other times they may be completely inappropriate. Jung also sensed a certain inexhaustibility of psychic contents of the unconscious. He wrote,

> This personal unconscious rests upon a deeper layer which does not derive from personal experience and is not a personal acquisition but is inborn. This deeper layer I call the collective unconscious. I have chosen the term "collective" because this part of the unconscious is not individual but universal; in contrast to the personal psyche, it has contents and modes of behavior that are more or less the same everywhere and in all individuals. It is identical in all men and thus constitutes a common psychic substrate of a suprapersonal nature which is present in every one of us.[8]

When Jung refers to the collective unconscious, we are by his definition and our definition outside the purview of the Psycho-Personal Approach, and within the Socio-Cultural and Transpersonal-Spiritual contexts. We have reserved a separate discussion of it in the latter two approaches.

At this point, we see that Jung defines at least a part of "the unconscious" in terms of repressed material.

## OTTO RANK

Otto Rank extends the discussion of the content of the repressed material further back in time in an individual's life. Freud emphasized the oedipal period, Jung called attention to the pre-oedipal period. With Rank, we will consider a man who contended that our birth experience was the beginning point of the unconscious.

The story that Rank tells is one of paradise, paradise lost, and paradise regained. "Paradise" refers to those nine months we all spend in our mother's womb. We lost that paradise at birth and are now spending the rest of our lives trying to recover that state of bliss. Rank expressed the sum of his theory as "the fundamental importance of the birth trauma, its repression and its return in neurotic reproductions, symbolic adaptation, heroic compensation, ethical reaction formation, aesthetic idealization, and philosophic speculation."[9] He made the point clear that the trauma of birth has suffered the most intense repression. Because of its painfulness, we never want to repeat it, but yet we forever seek what we have lost.

Otto Rank made some direct and rather bold statements regarding the unconscious, the birth trauma, and analysis. He contended that "after a thorough examination of the Unconscious . . . we have come up against the final origin of the psychical unconscious in the psycho-physical . . . the birth trauma the ultimate biological basis of the psychical . . . the nucleus of the Unconscious."[10] Rank argued that because of this discovery "analysis is now in the position to free itself to an extensive degree from the work of investigation."[11] From Rank's viewpoint if the birth trauma is so central to a person's psychological development then we already know what to look for. For Rank the birth trauma is the beginning, middle, and end. The psychotherapist need not search for other causes but simply look for the manifestations and so forth related to the primal trauma.

The preceding statements by Otto Rank are provocative considering that he is dealing with a time in our lives of which we have almost no certain knowledge. Rank made much use of the capitalized noun form of the word "unconscious." The implication in his writing is that the Unconscious is a kind of second self or some It.

With Otto Rank we have completed this presentation of theorists who had an understanding of the unconscious as the function of repression, although they differed somewhat on the nature of the repressed material.

## Alternative Constructs: The Unconscious Reinterpreted in Terms of Self-Deception, The Unverbalized, Figure-Ground, The Positive, and the Hidden

The plan here is to present other theories about what the unconscious refers to. These theorists reject the interpretations that we have just presented, that is, the unconscious in terms of the repressed. They also reject the implication that the unconscious is a place or thing. In general they believe that they offer a better understanding of why a person behaves as he does, without speaking in terms of the unconscious or repression.

## Self-Deception

The construct of the unconscious is rejected, and in its place the phenomenon of self-deception is offered as a better way to understand the behavior in question. Some of the theorists who share this point of view include: Jean-Paul Sartre, Mark Conkling, Rhawn Joseph, and William Stekel.

Freud maintained that between the unconscious and the conscious operated a censor that protected consciousness from unacceptable material contained in the unconscious. The operation of this censor is carried out unconsciously, that is, supposedly the ego has no idea of what the censor is doing or that it is doing anything. Repression is the technical term used to describe this mechanism. When a patient said "I don't know x, y, or z," Freud contended that patients said it right—they did not know. The essence of the counter-argument here is that the patient *does know* and is really saying, "I don't want to know."

Jean-Paul Sartre thought that it was disturbing enough that Freud distinguished between the conscious and the unconscious thereby cutting the psyche into two. The further differentiation of a censor only served to fragment the psyche into three parts.[12] The person so fragmented is left with a conscious one identifies with, an unconscious one does not know about, and a censor that also one does not know about, but which apparently knows the person better than one knows oneself. It is ironic that Freud, in trying to bridge the gap between consciousness and behavior by postulating an unconscious, also created another gap between conscious and unconscious. This gap he tried to fill with his construct of the censor but succeeded in creating still another gap, this time between the unconscious and the censor and the censor and the conscious. In short, Freud, in his efforts to find continuity in human events, also created discontinuities within the human psyche.

It is understandable that Sartre, as a philosophical existentialist, would recoil at the implications of a construct of the unconscious. The Freudian formulation leads to a determinism in human affairs that threatens the very heart of the existentialist's endeavor, namely, the advocacy of individual freedom and responsibility. What was Sartre's alternative explanation?

Sartre contended that the censor must know what it is repressing, precisely in order not to allow the repressed material from entering consciousness. Under these circumstances the person is in a state that Sartre referred to as "bad faith." The person on the one hand knows, or some thing in the person knows, what the person does not want to recognize, yet, on the other hand, the conscious awareness of the person appears to be denied access to the unacceptable material. In short, the person knows and does not know. Sartre contended that the person was really just indulging in self-deception and trying to ignore or refuse to pay close attention to certain responses.

Mark Conkling, in writing about this topic, stated explicitly the dilemma involved between Freud's and Sartre's positions. If we go along with the Freudian explanation, Sartre could say that we are deceiving ourselves and avoiding our responsibility. If we side with Sartre's view, Freud could say that we are are resisting because of the possible blow to our primary narcissism.[13] Conkling argued that Sartre's proposal was more parsimonious and preserved the concept of individual freedom. As we shall soon see, the issue is more involved than attempting to decide between repression or self-deception. First though we want to present the views of two more thinkers who conceptualized the unconscious in terms of the phenomenon of self-deception.

The psychologist Rhawn Joseph also emphasized the idea of self-deception. He contended that there is no acceptable evidence to indicate that ideas, feelings, and so forth are products or exist in the unconscious.[14] Joseph agreed with William Stekel, who claimed that patients were trying to deceive the psychotherapist and themselves. The contention here is that the patient does know but does not want to know.[15] For some reason the patient is pretending not to know something related to the problem in question.

In sum, what we have seen so far is that Sartre, Conkling, Joseph, and Stekel argued that the phenomenon of self-deception is a better analytic than the construct of the unconscious when trying to understand certain behaviors.

As we said a little earlier the issue is not as simple as just deciding between repression and self-deception. Some have suggested that neither position takes into account the possibility of genuine false perception and genuine error of judgment.[16] Others have pointed out that there are effective limits to self-knowledge.[17] Not all errors are lies. Still others have argued that repression is more like an illness than an act of bad will.[18] It is more a case of something happening to us than of our doing it consciously or unconsciously. Others have remarked that the act of keeping painful material from consciousness may be a natural self-protective mechanism of the personality.[19] In this case, this mechanism is like the reaction of shock which serves to insulate the person from physical pain. Finally, others argue that the construct of the unconscious, in the service of self-deception, makes sound evolutionary sense in that natural selection should favor a degree of self-deception.[20] Here we have an interesting mix of both a construct of the unconscious and the notion of self-deception. The idea is that sometimes, for survival or other motives, we need to deceive others and, to make the deception work (more believable), we need to fool ourselves.

If we remember the key question here, namely, why do people behave as they do, we have so far presented a series of possible answers. Freud offered his explanation in terms of a repressed unconscious. Sartre and others rejected this interpretation and argued in terms of the concept of self-deception as a better interpretation. But we also saw that there is more to deciphering human motivation than merely deciding between repression or deception.

## THE UNVERBALIZED

This next rejection of the construct of the unconscious involves the reinterpretation of it in terms of what can be put into words. In other words, when trying to explain behavior, rather than hypothesize some mysterious unconscious that operates in our lives, it is preferable to speak about 1) experiences that influence one's life but happened at a time before one could put the experience into words—*preverbal* experiences, or 2) experiences that influenced one's life but were not put into words for that person although they could have been—*unverbalized* experiences, or 3) experiences one might have which seem to be beyond words—*nonverbal* or *transverbal* experiences.

Because of the variety of theorists that will be presented in this section we want to make it clear what we are saying about them when they are grouped in this instance. They represent different schools of thought, but they have these things in common: 1) they wrote about the unconscious, and 2) they did so interpreting the construct in terms of what can or cannot, is or is not, put into words. They are presented as different expressions of this type of reinterpretation. These include the ideas of John B. Watson, Alfred Adler, Edward Sapir, John Anderson, Demetrios Papageorgis, Emil Froeschels, and, although we will not consider any one in particular, we will briefly mention the ideas of object relational psychologists.

## JOHN B. WATSON

John B. Watson, for the most part, belongs in the Bio-Physical Approach in the same section as that dealing with B. F. Skinner and the experimental psychologists. He is presented here only because of his explicit reference to the construct he called the "unverbalized."

Watson was probably the most outspoken critic of the construct of the unconscious. As the prototypical, classical behaviorist, Watson rejected any mentalistic constructs. He was particularly harsh on Freud. He referred to Freud's ideas as mysticism, voodooism, and vitalism. For Watson, there is no observable or inferable mind to get sick and there is no unconscious which can house and nurse festering psychic germs. Watson contended that "in place of the Freudian unconscious, the behaviorist substitutes the expression 'unverbalized.'"[21] Also, he went on to explain,

> When our word world does not equal our object world there is a residual unverbalized world. The "unconscious" (or unverbalized world) . . . is

that part of the individual's object world which he constantly manipu-
lates with his hands, feet, and body but does not name or attach a word
to—his world of situations and his own responses to them which he does
not name.[22]

Watson commented that no mystery needs to be made of this and that
no hypothesis of an unconscious or repression needed to be dragged
in.

Watson was a classical behaviorist, and, regarding the relationship
between behaviorism and a construct of the unconscious, J. D. Keehn
made two points. Although the behaviorists reject any kind of men-
talism, they do not reject unconscious processes. The behaviorists
contend that they can account for behavior sometimes attributed to
the working of an unconscious mind by reference to a particular
history of reinforcement of an activity, and whatever verbal behavior
is used to justify the activity is also shown to be acquired through an
independent reinforcement history of its own.[23]

The second point Keehn made was that, because the neurotic
cannot give an acceptable verbal account of his present behavior and
the normal individual can, some tend to attribute the former's behavior to unconscious factors and the latter's behavior to conscious ones.
In fact, this is precisely what Freud did. But, to a behaviorist, all
behavior is a function of particular histories of reinforcement. The
distinction between conscious and unconscious, from this point of
view, is arbitrary and need not be entertained at all.[24] Ironically,
both Freud and Watson worked with histories and behavior, but each
took very different postures toward these things.

## ALFRED ADLER (JOHN ANDERSON AND EDWARD SAPIR)

Alfred Adler will be presented in two places in this chapter (see
section entitled "The Hidden"). Here, we will consider only what he
said about the unverbalized. He wrote,

The child builds up his whole life at a time when he has neither adequate
language nor adequate concepts. Also he grows in a movement which has
never been formulated into words and therefore, unassailable to crit-

icism, is also withdrawn from the criticism of experience. We cannot say that this is a repressed unconscious . . . rather . . . that something has not been understood or something has been withheld from the understanding.[25]

Adler did not want to employ the construct of the unconscious.

This idea of the child growing up without the adequate self-understanding in terms of being able to put it into words, was also expressed by the sociologists Edward Sapir and John Anderson.[26]

## DEMETRIOS PAPAGEORGIS

Demetrios Papageorgis, an Adlerian, discussed eight alternative ways to explain the phenomenon of repression without recourse to the construct of the unconscious.[27] This is a landmark piece of writing because he assembled most of the relevant sources on the subject of repression and the unconscious. All of the alternatives that he suggested have either already been presented under the Bio-Physical Approach (automatic behavior, subliminal events, and memory processes) or are discussed in this or other sections of this chapter, such as the one treating the topic of self-deception.

One of those alternatives is a paraphrase of what we just read in reference to Adler. Papageorgis referred to this as the "incomplete assimilation of experience." His point was that a child perceives less, knows less, understands less, and labels less than the average adult. Closely related to this is another alternative which has to do with memory losses. The failure to recall certain material is not necessarily due to repression, which is sometimes referred to as "motivated forgetting." He suggested other reasons for this. Papageorgis wrote,

> The lack of verbal labels at the time of the event may make later recall difficult. When adults finally admit to experiences previously "unknown" to them, it is more appropriate to view them as applying new constructions to their self-concept than as demonstrating a new awareness of a fact forgotten long ago.[28]

On this last point, Papageorgis joins a host of others who argue along the same lines. These others include K. Koffka, Alfred Adler, Jean

Piaget, and so forth. They rejected the conception that memories act like submarines that can sink and surface at will and remain intact every time. They contended instead that we reconstruct as much as remember our past experiences.

Finally, another of the alternatives that Papageorgis presented was what he called "The Unavailability and Lack of Precision of Verbal Labels." Simply put, this refers to the fact that sometimes we do not have the right word to describe a situation or condition, and sometimes there may be a certain confusion of words in reference to one event or condition. Any difficulty or disagreement in communication or understanding regarding oneself or others does not necessarily mean that repression is involved.

## Object Relations Theory

The following brief remarks do not do justice to the field of object relational psychology, but the point we want to make can be made without going into much detail.

Object relational psychologists generally do not employ the expression "the unconscious." This is the chief reason why we have not presented this piece with any one theorist in mind. What object relational theorists (e.g., Melanie Klein, Ronald Fairbairn, Michael Balint, and Donald Winnicott) would consider to be the unconscious, or referred to by that expression, are those preverbal, pre-oedipal patternings that emerged out of the loosely structured, poorly differentiated interactions between the infant and the mothering one. In short, object relations theorists are saying that from the time of conception (Winnicott would include even the prenatal period) until the time when we are able to begin to verbalize our experiences, we already had had many experiences which, although we have not understood them, influence our behavior. The patternings that were so formed may be considered our unconscious, but these theorists prefer not to use that expression.

## Emil Froeschels

Emil Froeschels, unlike the theorists presented so far, did not actually reject the concept of the unconscious but merely wanted to substitute other words for it. He is included here because the nature of his substitutions was centered on the notion of the verbal. His proposal was to replace the expressions "conscious" with "expression-ripe," "preconscious" with "nearly expression-ripe," and "unconscious" with "not-expression-ripe." By "expression" he included such forms of expression as speech, music, sculpture, and, in general, all the fine arts. He also made reference to what he called the "not-speech-ripe organ" and "not-speech-ripe region" of our personality. He endowed these with a certain autonomy, wisdom, and ability to create both symptoms and artistic productions.[29]

What we have in Froeschels' case is an attempt to give the Freudian unconscious a new name but not necessarily a new understanding.[30] The other theorists that we have discussed did want to provide a new understanding. They wanted to redefine it, not in terms of some thing in the person that operates to prevent painful material from reaching consciousness, but to argue that it is more the case that we do not have access to many of our experiences (good or bad) simply because they were preverbal, unverbalized, or unable to be articulated adequately.

Here, in the Psycho-Personal Approach, we find a replay of the issue raised in the Bio-Physical Approach concerning the relationship between the unconscious and the ability to verbalize. In the latter approach, we saw that some wanted to make the distinction between conscious and unconscious a function of language ability and conclude that the left (verbal) hemisphere is the seat of consciousness and the right (nonverbal) hemisphere is the seat of unconsciousness. Here, in the Psycho-Personal Approach, we are not dealing with hemispheres, but the argument is essentially the same, that is, to distinguish conscious and unconscious along the lines of a verbal factor. There is no problem in doing this provided that it is made clear that these distinctions are made by definition only, that is, a definition of consciousness in terms of the verbal factor. Such a definition is purely an arbitrary one. Also, if one is referring to preverbal or unverbalized experiences, it seems superfluous to use the expression "the unconscious" in relation to those experiences. It would be less ambiguous to drop the expression "unconscious" and simply speak in terms of preverbal and unverbalized experiences.

### FIGURE-GROUND PHENOMENA

Theorists who make use of the figure-ground model reject the dichotomous model of the psyche proposed by Sigmund Freud, Carl Jung, and Otto Rank. These latter three pictured the psyche as one split into two major layers—conscious and unconscious. Figure-ground theorists would rather conceive of the psyche as a continuous whole in which the conscious and unconscious are not separable distinctions, but rather are two aspects of one totality that have a fluid relationship with one another. Conscious and unconscious are not strict categories that endure, but are both relative aspects that can interchange depending on the situation. To derive a sense of what this means and how it works, let us consider the famous faces-or-vase picture.

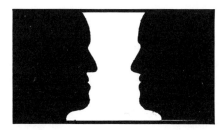

When we look at the picture, sometimes we see the middle vase and at other times we see two profiles. Unless one concentrates on one or the other, one will see spontaneous and frequent reversals between the two images. Each image serves as the background for the other. In a sense, we can say that, in one instance, the vase is unconscious (not in immediate awareness) while the profiles are in consciousness. In another instance, the positions are reversed. In sum, this paradigm has been offered as another way to understand some of the phenomena which are sometimes assigned to the agency of the unconscious.

We will now consider some theorists who relied on the figure-ground model as a counter-proposal to the conscious-unconscious model of Freud and others. The principles underpinning this alternative are derived mainly from gestalt psychology. Indeed the figure-ground relationship is one of the main features of this type of psychology.

Rex Collier once wrote that the figure-ground model denies the antagonistic relationship between conscious and unconscious that the Freudian model assumed. The former model insists on a certain continuity between the two psychic aspects, and sees the relationship between conscious and unconscious as supportive. If we consider our faces-vase illustration, we would not say that the profiles are in conflict with the vase for attention, rather, we would say that they provide one another with context.

Collier also argued that the Freudian conceptualizations by implication destroyed the autonomous individuality of the person.[31] He was disturbed by the statement made by Freud to the effect that the ego is not the master of its own house. In reacting as he did to this remark, Collier revealed his own presumption about the autonomous individuality of the person. In the ideological war over the image of the human of which both Freud and Collier are a part, the latter is on the side of those who prefer to conceive a human being as an undivided whole and as possessing autonomy.

In his investigation, John Welwood relied heavily on the figure-ground model. He made a good point when he commented,

> We do not speak of *the* conscious, so why then speak of *the* unconscious? . . . This study [referring to his thesis] is seeking to replace the notion of *the* unconscious, through phenomenological analysis, with the notion of organismic structurings of the world which functions as the ground of focal attention. . . . What is unconscious are the many ways in which the whole organism functions as a structuring background to focal attention.[32]

In another place Welwood suggested that the preconscious, personal unconscious, and collective unconscious were really levels of structuring, more-or-less accessible and more-or-less affecting functioning, but they did not represent realms.[33] Welwood, like Collier, also felt that the figure-ground model promoted a more continuous and fluid relationship between conscious and unconscious without connoting a split image of the human being's psychic structure.

The last person to mention is Erich Fromm. Although he did not articulate his ideas explicitly in terms of figure and ground, he did stress the point about the relativity of the constructs conscious and unconscious. He remarked,

> The "unconscious" is the unconscious only in relation to the "normal" state of activity. . . . But the day world is as unconscious in our sleep experience as the night world is in our waking experience . . . both conscious and unconscious are only different states of mind referring to different states of existence. [34]

Here again we get a sense of the fluid nature of the two categories in question.

To conclude, with the figure-ground model, we understand two things: 1) the construct of the unconscious as an entity, place, or system is rejected; 2) the image of the psyche as made up of parts is rejected. These are rejected in favor of a very relative understanding of what is conscious and what is unconscious. It depends on what aspect, at a given moment, functions as the focus, with the other aspect automatically serving as the background.

## THE POSITIVE

Those theorists such as Sigmund Freud and Otto Rank, who understood the unconscious in terms of repression, gave the unconscious a negative description. They conceived of it as a place where unacceptable, painful, and disturbing thoughts, feeling, impulses, and so forth reside and exert constant pressure on consciousness. Now, by talking about the unconscious in terms of the positive, we are considering a point of view that takes exception to the strictly negative view of it. Generally speaking, representatives of humanistic psychology are the ones who promote a more positive interpretation of the unconscious. These theorists include such people as Abraham Maslow, Carl Rogers, Rollo May, and others. They contended that neither behaviorism nor psychoanalysis did justice to the understanding of a healthy and creatively functioning person. Regarding the construct of the unconscious, they argued that it represented much more than merely the dark cellar of the psyche from which undesirable material emerges. One can trust the unconscious to be a creative force in one's life rather than as something to be always feared.

Representatives of humanistic psychology contend that the construct of the repressed unconscious lends itself to a dualism, mechanism, and reductionism, and to being reified. They argue that the idea of a hidden reality working behind the scenes of consciousness is not acceptable and prefer to conceptualize conscious and unconscious on equal terms, as two aspects of one whole, and both aspects working toward one goal. In this last point we hear echoes of figure-ground thinking as well as Adlerian lines of thought.

Ronald Scolastico said it well when he remarked that humanistic psychology has "freed the unconscious from its taint of pathology, of irrationality, of immaturity, and primitiveness."[35] The image of the unconscious as a disruptive, alien, and negative force gives way to an image of it as a referent for all those positive, growth-orientated, creative impulses emerging from the depths of the human being.

Abraham Maslow expressed this point of view:

> The roots of all mental health were found first in the unconscious; it has been the tendency to think of the unconscious as bad, evil, crazy, dirty, or dangerous, and to think of the primary process as distorting the truth. But now we have found these depths to be also the source of creativeness, of art, of love, of humor, and play, and even certain kinds of truth and knowledge.[36]

Rollo May made this remark:

> I define the unconscious as the potentialities for awareness, experience, and action which the individual up to that moment cannot or will not actualize.[37]

May added in a footnote that the word "unconscious" was to be used as a shorthand expression, that it did not mean *the* unconscious, but rather referred to unconscious dimensions, levels, aspects, or sources of experiences.[38]

To sum up this point of view, we can say that the image of the disruptive unconscious gives way to the image of the creative unconscious. We no longer ask, "what is it hiding" but, "what is it trying to unfold?"

## THE HIDDEN

We will consider here the ideas of Alfred Adler and Joseph Kockelmans. The former is the founder of Individual Psychology; the latter is a spokesman for Daseinsanalysis. Both men, and the schools they represent, took exception to the Freudian understanding of the unconscious and offered reformulations. We have given these men a separate section because they made use of the expression "hidden" in reference to the unconscious. Because of this they offered another nuance of meaning regarding what is meant by the unconscious.

## ALFRED ADLER

Alfred Adler was once a follower of Freud but broke away. Two theoretical and one practical considerations, relative to the construct of the unconscious, were among the reasons why Adler broke with Freud.

Regarding theory, Adler differed from Freud in that, whereas the latter posited the unconscious as a separate sphere of influence in conflict with consciousness, Adler understood an unconscious that is the lower end of an awareness continuum and not fundamentally in conflict with consciousness. Adler also differed from Freud regarding the contents of the unconscious. Freud claimed to have found sexually-toned repressed material; Adler claimed to have found misguided strivings for power.

The practical point of difference between Adler and Freud has to do with psychotherapy. Adler thought that the construct of the unconscious can be an easy temptation for a patient to appeal to in order to avoid responsibility. It can be used as an excuse for what one is or is not, and what one does or has done. Without such a construct, the patient has no recourse but to face the problem as one's own. Adler avoided the use of the construct of the unconscious and, in its place, preferred to talk about what is not understood or what is hidden from self-awareness. We might add that he wanted to avoid any tendency toward reification to which the construct of the unconscious easily lends itself.[39]

How Adler explained what he meant by the unconscious is best understood in the context of some of his basic assumptions. Adler assumed that all of us have a life-plan, a life-goal, and a lifestyle. Essentially, what can be considered the unconscious are the aspects of our life-plan, goal, and style that we are not aware of and do not yet understand. We can say that they are hidden from us. A major reason we do not understand is that we may never have had the words for understanding. Here we have an echo of what was said earlier regarding the unverbalized. The last point here is that the hidden aspects we just mentioned are never considered as separate parts, realms, things, and so forth.[40]

Adler assumed the unity of the personality and argued that everything connected with that personality is a part of that unity and in the service of that unity. A corollary of this major assumption provides the key to how Adler would interpret behavior. The supreme law operating, as he saw it, is that the sense of worth of the self shall not be allowed to be diminished.[41] This is so important to people that they will live a lie or deceive themselves for the sake of maintaining self-esteem. These considerations tend to support Sartre's notion of "self-deception" to the extent that they provide some reason why a person would want to deceive themselves.

Adler contended that, because conscious-unconscious are not contradictory but form a unity, the methods used in interpreting conscious material may be used to interpret unconscious material. Every response of the person manifests one's lifestyle, and one's lifestyle determines one's behavior. We can never escape our lifestyle.

In sum, Adler joins the representatives of the figure-ground model and others in rejecting the split-image of the psyche. Adler argued for an image of the person and psyche as a whole, a unity in which every aspect is an expression of that unity. All that can be referred to as unconscious has to do with what the person has not yet understood about the unity that one is. Under this condition, it can be said that something is hidden from the person.

## Joseph Kockelmans

As a spokesman for phenomenological Daseinsanalysis, Joseph Kockelmans wrote an article directly related to our subject and, in it, introduced the key people of this way of thinking.[42] He explained that Daseinsanalysis is a school of thought inspired by Martin Heidegger, originated by Ludwig Binswanger, and developed further by Medard Boss. As a theory of the human, those who expounded it want to understand the person as a totality, a unity, and as a being-in-the-world. This system of ideas rejects any approach or treatment of the person as if they were a machine with malfunctioning parts or a sick organism. Also, Daseinsanalysts take exception to the construct of the unconscious and find it unacceptable because it gives the impression that some thing is operating in the conscious personality as if it were a second person.[43] The person is to be understood and approached only as a totality, not as a summation of regions, systems, or layers.

Despite the preceding comments, some, like Binswanger, realized that what Freud called the unconscious does refer to an important dimension in the person. In Daseinsanalysis, this dimension is referred to as one's "thrownness and facticity." This Heideggerian expression Binswanger explained as the given conditions of one's life which limit, define, and determine us. These can include the fact that we have a physical body, a past, a culture, and a character.[44] In short, it includes everything that makes up our background and the context of our life. Of course, many of these conditions are not always clearly understood by us or are hidden from our immediate awareness. Kockelmans wrote,

> As the science of phenomena, phenomenology must assume that in what shows itself first and foremost (phenomena), there is something that at first is still hidden, that this hidden meaning can be brought to light by phenomenological analysis and interpretation, and finally that what is so brought to light constitutes the "truth" of what showed itself originally. Thus, all conscious awareness implies a reference to something hidden, "unconscious."[45]

Daseinsanalysts contend that all the phenomena to which Freud referred to prove the existence of the unconscious can be explained without appealing to that construct. Such phenomena as parapraxes, dreams, and so forth, should be understood as being related to certain actual or possible modes of one's being-in-the-world.[46] Kockelmans made this claim:

> Daseinsanalysis is capable of explaining all symptoms of psychic and mental illness as flowing from the typical manner in which each patient relates to his world.[47]

In other words, it is important to find out first what ontology the patient is living with before one can make sense of the patient's behavior. This ontology may be hidden, that is, the patient may not be aware of it or simply cannot see it.

Binswanger used other expressions for what we can call "hidden ontology." He referred to the "Existential A Priori," "horizon of experience," and "transcendental experiential horizon." These relate to the meaning context of an individual that makes one's experience possible as one's experience. We can say that the person sees by these contexts but may not see or realize that one is using them. Binswanger wrote,

> The Existential A Priori makes possible the effect of the past on the present; the relation of the present individual to his past is not itself determined by that past, but by the horizon within which he experiences both present and past.[48]

For example, it is not correct to say that A (in the past) causes B (now), but rather that C (the person's ontology) made both A and B possible. C must change in order to change the behavior in question. This is a very different approach from the one Freud used. He sought to trace the long chains of causes back to the original cause. For Freud, the past strictly determines the present.

Besides the distinction we just alluded to between psychoanalysis and Daseinsanalysis, there is another more radical distinction between the two. With the former, the psychoanalysts work with essentially one ontology—the psychoanalytic worldview, and attempt to apply it to everyone or fit everyone into it. One ontology is accepted and everyone must be reeducated into it. With Daseinsanalysis, no reeducation or psychotherapy can begin until the analyst has comprehended the unique ontology of the patient. Without that grasp of the "typical manner a person relates to his world," the Daseinsanalyst cannot make a diagnosis or a prognosis. Each patient represents and lives in and out of a different worldview. From this point of view, Daseinsanalysis a radical approach. It does not really have a theory of personality except one conceived along very broad and general lines. In a sense, the Daseinsanalyst encounters the patient as a virtual extra-terrestrial—as one from another "world." Such a radical approach represents a radical respect for the individual. One wonders, though, how it actually works in the therapeutic situation.

One more point needs to be mentioned, and this has to do with the placing of Adlerian psychology and Daseinsanalysis in this section. The common denominator between the two is more than just the fact that both describe the unconscious in terms of the hidden. When one thinks about it, there does not seem to be that great a difference between talking about "lifestyles" and "modes of being-in-the-world." In a sense, one could say that they are referring to the same thing. This is at best a superficial appraisal and needs to be looked into more carefully.

This paragraph should be considered an appendix to this section on the unconscious and the hidden. It is related to the ideas of Martin Buber and Ronald Romanyshyn, who also spoke on behalf of Jacques Merleau-Ponty. They are omitted in the main body of this typology because their ideas on the unconscious simply do not fit any of the approaches. They spoke of an unconscious, if we use Romanyshyn's words, that "surrounds conscious life, an unconsciousness in the world, between us."[49] Buber would speak of it as the ground or state of relationship that is always present, a condition between and not in people.[50] If this understanding of unconscious had to be fitted within the typology, it could be squeezed into this section on the nuance of hiddenness regarding the unconscious. We say this because the immediacy of experience or of relationship, that they have alluded to, is difficult to see, and because every reflection about immediacy is always a reflection within immediacy. Immediacy always is and usually taken for granted. We said "squeezed" earlier because these theorists would reject any psycho-personal type of unconscious. It is the intent of doing this typological study not to leave any point of view out. This seems to be the best place to mention this particular point of view.

This ends our discussion of the alternative ways that have been offered in the attempt to reinterpret the construct of the unconscious away from the strict psychoanalytic appropriation of it.

## Cognitive Functions and the Unconscious

The Freudian unconscious is largely of an affective nature. It is charged with energy, and composed of impulses looking for objects, outlets, and expression. We will now consider two theorists who did not necessarily argue with Freud, but who did expand the area of what is subsumed under the construct of the unconscious to include cognitive operations. The two main figures in this section are Jean Piaget and Claude Levi-Strauss.

### JEAN PIAGET

Jean Piaget understood the construct of the unconscious to be a very general expression that involved much more than the emotional life of an individual.[51] The substance of his ideas on the topic were taken from his address at the plenary session of the American Psychoanalytic Association in 1970. In one section of his address he compared and contrasted the affective and cognitive dimensions of the unconscious. Whereas affectivity is characterized by an energetic component, the cognitive aspect is characterized by structures.[52] Both aspects are to be considered components of the unconscious.

The heart of his message, for our purposes, is contained in the following remarks:

The deepest functioning of the intelligence remains entirely unknown to the subject until we reach some rather high level where reflection on this problem of structures becomes possible. Until then, the thoughts of the subject are directed by structures whose existence is unknown to him. . . . The cognitive unconscious thus consists in an ensemble of structures and of functions unknown by the subject except in their results. There was profound truth in Binet's whimsical expression: "Thought is an unconscious activity of the mind."[53]

Besides drawing the parallel between the affective unconscious and the cognitive unconscious, Piaget proposed another analogy, this time between affective repression and what he called "cognitive repression." What he meant by that was that a child may be able to perform some action but may not have all the verbal labels to fully describe the action, so the child will distort or even ignore certain aspects of the action in order to make sense of the action at the child's level of understanding.

In reference to past memories, Piaget was against the "submarine" theory of memory and in favor of an understanding of memory that considers all acts of recall as involving a reorganization of the recalled material. He wrote that "memory works like a historian who reconstructs the past, in part deductively, on the basis of documents which are always to some extent incomplete."[54] Because of this and the fact of the existence of false memories, Piaget cautioned against the use of childhood memories as "hard" facts.

Piaget concluded that affective and cognitive mechanisms mutually determine and influence one another, that they always remain interrelated though distinct. This goes without saying if the former are based on energies and the latter on structures.

## CLAUDE LEVI-STRAUSS

Claude Levi-Strauss, the structural anthropologist, also understood the unconscious to involve more than just affective elements. Like Piaget, he also used the term "structure" but in a different way. Piaget's "structures" are acquired, while those of Levi-Strauss are innate. There are other differences as we shall soon learn. In general though, we can say that both men understood the unconscious to refer to the lack of awareness of certain mechanisms or laws governing certain behaviors. With Piaget we would include mechanisms governing intellectual behavior, with Levi-Strauss we would include laws governing group or individual behavior in general.

Between Claude Levi-Strauss and Sigmund Freud there is a significant difference of opinion regarding the unconscious. We can highlight the differences by making the following comparisons:

The Unconscious

| For Freud | For Levi-Strauss |
|---|---|
| Was a function of instinctual energy and the conceptual component is its derivative | Was a function of the permanent and logical structures of the mind |
| Was emotional in nature | Was intellectual |
| Involved affective motivation | Involved logical structures |
| Its contents include: affects, sensations, impulses, feelings, and wishes | Was made up of forms without contents |

Now that we have outlined the major differences between the two theorists, we want to understand how Levi-Strauss explained what he meant by the construct of the unconscious. The closest that we can come to a definition is this:

> The unconscious activity of mind imposes structures upon physical and psychic context. The aggregate of these structures constitute the unconscious.[55]

The question of the ontological status of Levi-Strauss' unconscious is a major problem in trying to locate him neatly within this typological study. The structures that he wrote about are understood to be not only unconscious, but universal, autonomous, and independent of the individual involved. By definition, it appears that he should be considered under the Transpersonal-Spiritual Approach. The

Psycho-Personal Approach deals with a personal, personally historic, and subject-dependent understanding of the unconscious. The complexity of this issue of where to place him is compounded by another aspect of his understanding of structures.

The argument could be made that Levi-Strauss should have been presented under the Bio-Physical Approach. This is so because his construct of the unconscious is ultimately a function of the brain structures (precisely the binary, oppositional mode of functioning of the brain). So why is he presented in the Psycho-Personal Approach? One reason for this is that he, like Piaget, dealt with structures as opposed to emotions, and thereby his ideas serve to expand the purely affective tone of the unconscious set by Freud. Levi-Strauss is presented here for contrast.

Second, concerning the bio-physical point, it can be said that his writings are not full of anatomical terms and discussions. After all, he was an anthropologist, not a biologist. Also, regarding the transpersonal aspect, he did not convey an idea of the unconscious as being some kind of an entity. His subject matter was people's customs, rituals, and language behavior. With all these points taken into account, we will leave Levi-Strauss here but admit that he does not sit well here.

The hypothesis of anthropological structuralism is that unconscious structures underlie cultural phenomena. Levi-Strauss claimed to have discovered unconscious infrastructures which regulate the unconscious activity of the mind, which determines the ordering capacity of language, which, in turn, influences the formation of concepts, ideas, and systems of thought (the superstructures). Levi-Strauss contended that, with his discovery of these structures, he had a key to interpret customs and institutions and could give intelligibility to apparently hetergeneous and hard to understand social phenomena.[56]

Ino Rossi in commenting on the ideas of Levi-Strauss argued that the latter did not advocate a wholesale, physical reductionism, but instead was arguing for an isomorphism of mental, social, and physical laws.[57] It appears that Rossi is drawing a fine line here between reductionism and isomorphism.

To conclude, with Jean Piaget and Claude Levi-Strauss we have an expansion of what can be considered unconscious to include more than just affective elements. However, with Piaget it would be more descriptive to talk about the deep, subtle functioning of intelligence; and, with Levi-Strauss, to talk about universal patterns of apperception rather than to speak in terms of the unconscious. In other words, by dropping the word "unconscious" (noun form) from their writings, we would lose very little, except a possible misunderstanding of the use of the expression.

## Conclusion

In the Bio-Physical Approach, the construct of the unconscious was said to be sometimes associated with memory processes, conditioning, physiological activity, automatism, and subthreshold events. The use of the noun form of the word "unconscious" with these items is a source of confusion. In fact, we argued that the construct of the unconscious has been confused with these other phenomena and need not be.

In the Psycho-Personal Approach, we followed a different plan than with the Bio-Physical Approach. We were not so concerned to discuss the confusion of the notion, but to present a variety of interpretations concerning what the expression "unconscious" refers to.

We opened with an understanding of the unconscious as a function of repressed material. This interpretation was promoted by Freud, Jung, and Rank. They made extensive use of the noun form of the word "unconscious." It is precisely this noun-form usage that has proven problematic, and for two main reasons. One, the noun form gives the impression that some thing, entity, or place is being referred to. Two, the acceptance of some thing operating in the person implies an image of the person as one body with two entities. It was in reaction to this reification and fragmentation that other theorists came forth with their reformulations and alternative accounts of behavior in terms other than repression. The directions that these alternatives have taken involve the use of such concepts as self-deception, the unverbalized, figure-ground, the positive, and the hidden. Those who have advocated these alternative constructs contended that they are a better way to understand behavior, that they maintain the presumed unity of the person and offset the purely negative tone given to the unconscious by advocates of the repressed model.

In a sense, we could rewrite the summary of the Psycho-Personal Approach by first posing the question: "Can one be unconscious of motives and/or behavior?" We could then assemble a series of answers that would represent the various points of view that we presented. For example:

1) Advocates of the repressed unconscious would answer that the patient can correctly say "I do not know."

2) Advocates of the self-deceptive model would say that it is not a case of not knowing, but more that the person does not want to know.

3) Advocates of the unverbalized model could say that it is none of the above but merely a case that the person does not or did not have the right words to articulate one's motives or behavior.

4) Advocates of the construct of the unconscious in terms of what is hidden could say that the person just does not understand yet or cannot see yet all that makes up the contents and contexts of one's life.

We could go on and on. Some would emphasize that the person in question is simply ignorant of some things or that one has misjudged. In short, there is more to the question than to simply infer that something called "the unconscious" is responsible for certain seemingly unexplainable behavior. In fact, all of the alternatives were offered precisely in order to understand behavior without necessarily having to appeal to a construct of the repressed unconscious.

It is difficult to determine which answer is the appropriate one. Given the complexity of human motivation and the complex matrix of conditions out of which we behave, only a variety of interpretations can do justice to the question "why do we do what we do?"

In the controversy over theories and images of the person, and the psychotherapies that have been developed to heal, some construct of the unconscious has been used virtually by all sides of the issues. This book can help to locate and relate the various understandings of the construct. Although we cannot say who is right, we can say that, regarding the construct of the unconscious itself, everything that has been studied and explained in terms of it has been explained without appealing to that construct. How adequate those alternative explanations are depends on who is being asked to accept them. The success record of any form of psychotherapy is not sufficient proof of any one interpretation. In the end, we are forced to respect the complexity of human motivation and behavior.

# Notes

1. S. David House, "Psychologies of the Unconscious," *Psychoanalytic Review* 15 (1928), p. 7.

2. Mario Rendon, "Structuralism in Psychoanalysis," *American Journal of Psychoanalysis* 39, no. 4 (1979), p. 345.

3. Sigmund Freud, *The Standard Edition of the Complete Psychological Works of Sigmund Freud*, ed. J. Strachey, vol. XIX: *The Ego and the Id* (London: The Hogarth Press, 1974), p. 15.

4. Freud, *Standard Edition*, vol. XI: "Five Lectures on Psychoanalysis," p. 27.

5. Henri Ellenberger, "The Unconscious Before Freud," *Bulletin of the Menninger Clinic* 21, no. 3 (1957), p. 14.

6. Jung's ideas relevant to the Bio-Physical Approach are too few to warrant a special treatment of them. Let this quote suffice to demonstrate his appreciation of the bio-physical aspect: "The deeper 'layers' of the psyche lose their individual uniqueness as they retreat farther and farther into darkness. 'Lower down,' . . . they approach the autonomous functional systems . . . until they are universalized and extinguished in the body's materiality." (Carl Jung, "Confrontation with the Unconscious," in *Memories, Dreams, Reflections* (New York: Vintage Books, 1961), pp. 401–2.)

7. Carl Jung, *The Collected Works of Carl Jung*, vol. 9, part 1: "Conscious, Unconscious, and Individuation" (Princeton, New Jersey: Princeton University Press, 1966), p. 284.

8. Jung, *Collected Works*, vol. 9, part 1: "Archetypes of the Collective Unconscious," pp. 3–4.

9. Otto Rank, *The Trauma of Birth* (New York: Robert Brunner, 1952), p. 195.

11. Ibid., p. 11.

12. Jean-Paul Sartre, "Bad Faith," in *Being and Nothingness* (New York: Philosophical Library, Inc., 1956), pp. 50–53.

13. Mark Conkling, "Sartre's Refutation of the Freudian Unconscious," *Review of Existential Psychology and Psychiatry* 8, no. 2 (1968), p. 100.

14. Rhawn Joseph, "Awareness, The Origin of Thought, and the Role of Conscious Self-Deception in Resistance and Repression," *Psychological Reports* 46 (1980), p. 776.

15. Ibid., p. 776.

16. Gustav Ichheiser, "On Freud's Blind Spots Concerning Some Obvious Facts," *Journal of Individual Psychology* 16 (1960), p. 50.

17. W. Ver Eecke, "Of Freud's Theory of Negation," *Man and World* 14 (1981), p. 111.

18. Konstantin Kolenda, "Unconscious Motives and Human Action," *Inquiry* 7 (1964), p. 4.

19. F. Bassin and A. Sherozia, "The Role of the Category of the Unconscious in the System of the Present-Day Scientific Knowledge of the Mind," paper delivered at the International Symposium on the Problem of the Unconscious, Tbilisi, USSR, 1979, p. 25.

20. Gary Leak and Steven Christopher, "Freudian Psychoanalysis and Sociobiology," *American Psychologist* 39, no. 3 (March 1982), p. 319.

21. John B. Watson, "The Myth of the Unconscious," *Harper's Magazine,* no. 155 (1927), p. 503.

22. John B. Watson, "The Unconscious of the Behaviorist," in *The Unconscious, A Symposium,* ed: C. M. Child (New York: Alfred A. Knopf, 1927), p. 96.

23. J. D. Keehn, "Behaviorism and the Unconscious," *Acta Psychologica* 26 (1967), p. 7.

24. Ibid., p. 77.

25. Alfred Adler, *The Individual Psychology of Alfred Adler,* ed. H. Ansbacher (New York: Basic Books, 1956), p. 191.

26. See Edward Sapir, "The Unconscious Patterning of Behavior in Society," and John Anderson, "The Genesis of Social Reactions in the Young Child," in *The Unconscious, A Symposium,* ed. C. M. Child (New York: Alfred A. Knopf, 1927), pp. 114–44, and pp. 69–90.

27. Demetrios Papageorgis, "Repression and the Unconscious: A Social Psychological Reformulation," *Journal of Individual Psychology* 21, no. 1 (1965), pp. 18–31.

28. Ibid., p. 22.

29. Emil Froeschels, "About the Name and Some Pathologic Functions of the Unconscious," *Journal of Clinical Psychopathology and Psychotherapy* 7 (1945), pp. 274–79.

30. On the same point, we could mention Sandor Rado, who substituted the expression "nonreporting organization of causative links between processes of which we are aware" for "unconscious mind." See Sandor Rado, "Mind, Unconscious Mind, and Brain," in *Psychoanalysis of Behavior* (New York: Grune & Stratton, 1956), pp. 180–85.

31. Rex Collier, "A Figure-Ground Model Replacing the Conscious-Unconscious Dichotomy," *Journal of Individual Psychology* 20 (1964), pp. 6ff.

32. John Welwood, "A Theoretical Re-Interpretation of the Concept of the Unconscious From a Humanistic and Phenomenological Perspective," unpublished doctoral dissertation, University of Chicago, 1974, pp. 60, 124.

33. Ibid., pp. 60–61.

34. Erich Fromm, *The Forgotten Language* (New York: Holt, Rinehart and Winston, 1951), p. 29. Fromm, in another place offered this definition of "unconscious":

"Our unconscious, that is, that part of our self which is excluded from the organized ego which we identify with our self, contains both the lowest and the highest, the worst and the best. The unconscious must neither be held in awe or with horror but in humility and with a profound sense of humor." (Erich Fromm, *Psychoanalysis and Religion* (New Haven, Connecticut: Yale University Press, 1950), p. 96. Fromm offered this neutral rendition to distinguish his view from the more negative image conveyed by Freud and the more positive image conveyed by Jung.

35. Ronald Scolastico, "Meaningful Communication and the Unconscious: Contribution of Humanistic Psychology," unpublished doctoral dissertation, University of Iowa, 1978, p. 139.

36. William Wallace, "Some Dimensions of Creativity," *Personnel Journal* 46, no. 7 (1967), part 1, p. 366. Quote from Abraham Maslow, *Toward a Psychology of Being*, p. 171.

37. Rollo May, "Creativity and the Unconscious," *Humanitas* 1, no. 3 (Winter 1966), p. 300.

38. Ibid., p. 301.

39. Alfred Adler, *The Individual Psychology of Alfred Adler*, ed. H. Ansbacker (New York: Basic Books, 1956), p. 267.

40. Arthur Nikelly, "The Adlerian Concept of the Unconscious in Psychotherapy," *Journal of Individual Psychotherapy* 22 (1966): p. 1.

41. Adler, *Individual Psychology of A. Adler*, p. 358.

42. Joseph Kockelmans, "Daseinsanalysis and Freud's Unconscious," *Review of Existential Psychology and Psychiatry* 16, no. 1 (1978–79), pp. 25ff.

43. Ibid., p. 32.

44. Ludwig Binswanger, "The Unconscious," in *Being-in-the-World*, trans. J. Needleman (New York: Harper & Row, 1963), pp. 97ff.

45. Kockelmans, "Daseinsanalysis and Freud's Unconscious," pp. 32–33.

46. Ibid., p. 26.

47. Ibid., p. 27.

48. Binswanger, *Being-in-the World*, p. 92.

49. Ronald Romanyshyn, "Phenomenology and Psychoanalysis: Contribution of Merleau-Ponty," *Psychoanalytic Review* 64, no. 2 (1977), p. 215.

50. Maurice Friedman, Introduction to *The Knowledge of Man*, by Martin Buber (London: G. Allen & Unwin, 1965).

51. Nathan Gould, "The Structure of Dialectical Reason: A Comparative

Study of Freud's and Levi-Strauss' Concept of Unconscious Mind," *Ethos* 6, no. 4 (1978), p. 191.

52. Jean Piaget, "The Affective Unconscious and the Cognitive Unconscious," *Journal of American Psychoanalytic Association* 21 (1973), p. 250.

53. Ibid., p. 251.

54. Ibid., p. 258.

55. Ino Rossi, "The Unconscious in the Anthropology of Claude Levi-Strauss," *American Anthropologist* 75, no. 1 (1973), p. 27.

56. Ibid., p. 42.

57. Ibid., p. 32.

Chapter IV

# Socio-Cultural Approach

## Introduction

The expression "Socio-Cultural" is the third major generic term of this typological study. It represents that aggregate of literature which discusses the construct of the unconscious as a function of peoples, groups, and races. The unconscious in this context is understood as something that happens when individuals group themselves for various reasons. The gathering and associating of people is the necessary condition for this type of unconscious to manifest itself. This type of unconscious has no preexistence or postexistence. It is strictly a function of people. The unconscious can also refer to that part of the individual psyche that is held in common. This too comes about as a result of people. In short, without people this type of unconscious does not exist. This point is underlined to distinguish this type from the transpersonal-spiritual type, which does have a certain independence, preexistence, and everlastingness about it.

When the word "unconscious" appears in this type of literature, it is almost always used in the noun form. This usage of the word implies that some invisible thing is being talked about. "It" can be in the form of an entity or a realm within the psyche.

The diverse neologisms that have been developed within this framework include the following:

Collective Unconscious     Inherited Conglomerate
Collective Preconscious     Collective Consciousness
Common Unconscious          Herd Instincts

| | |
|---|---|
| National Soul | Racial Unconscious |
| Phalanx | Collective Psyche |
| The Family | Master Mind |

There is another idea, besides our definition, that helps to gain an overall perspective regarding the diverse viewpoints within this approach. This idea is borrowed from general systems theory. Simply stated, it states that the whole is more than the sum of its parts and that the whole determines the nature of the parts. Most of the following theorists explicitly or implicitly worked with this principle. This whole-part paradigm helps to unify the various ideas contained herein and supports the socio-cultural definition of the unconscious.

The plan of the presentation is to first present explicit examples of this type. This includes theorists who used the word "unconscious" (noun form) directly. Next we will consider implicit examples of this type. These are theorists who alluded to a construct of the unconscious in an indirect way by employing some other expression that could be translated as "the unconscious." We then will consider two types of rejection of the socio-cultural definition. One rejection originates from a sociological orientation, and the other from a political context.

In considering the Socio-Cultural Approach, we make a major shift in our attention. We are now not so concerned about what goes on within one person as we were in the previous two approaches, but with what is going on around, between, and above the single individual. We are concerned with a social understanding of what the unconscious means.

## Explicit Examples of the Socio-Cultural Type

### THE CROWD

Gustave LeBon's book *The Crowd* was at one time a well-known body of observations regarding the singular behavior of people when they formed groups. Today, his ideas are rarely mentioned in books on group behavior. What is of particular interest to us here is how LeBon understood the construct of the unconscious.

Before we discuss his ideas, it would be appropriate to have some sense of what LeBon meant by "crowd." He was not referring to any haphazard, occasional collection of people. He was referring to those collections or groupings of people with some reason, besides chance, to be so grouped. He considered different classifications of crowds. He distinguished heterogeneous crowds from homogeneous ones. The former include anonymous crowds like street crowds and those not anonymous like juries or governmental assemblies. The homogeneous type include political and religious sects; castes such as military and working castes; and classes such as the middle class or the peasant class. [1] In general, the idea is that the more factors that serve to unite a certain group or crowd, the more likely it will tend to respond as one body and manifest the singular phenomenon that LeBon was alluding to, that is, the transformation of the individual in the service of the collective.

LeBon began his book with these comments:

> Under certain given circumstances, and only under those circumstances, an agglomeration of men presents new characteristics very different from those of the individuals composing it. The sentiments and ideas of all the persons in the gathering take one and the same direction, and their conscious personality vanishes. *A collective mind is formed,* doubtless transitory, but presenting very clearly defined characteristics. The gathering has thus become what, in the absence of a better expression, I will call an organized crowd, or, if the term is considered preferable, a psychological crowd. *It forms a single being,* and is subjected to the law of the mental unity of crowds (emphasis added). [2]

LeBon offered very little in the way of explanation for such behavior. There is little theoretical discussion in the book. He devoted most of the work to describing the various features of group behavior. He did, though, make the following remark in the way of explanation:

> Our conscious acts are the outcome of an unconscious substratum created in the mind in the main by hereditary influences. This substratum

consists of the innumerable common characteristics handed down from generation to generation, which constitute the genius of a race.[3]

What he was implying is that, in a crowd situation, the unconscious substratum or racial unconscious surfaces and overshadows and neutralizes the individualistic aspects of the persons involved. In short, we can say that the person is no longer an individual but Humanity. In a quasi-magical way the individual life is suspended and in a quasi-mystical way, it merges with others so transformed to form a single being.

We will proceed with this discussion by considering Freud's objection to LeBon's analysis, and Jung's affinity with LeBon's assessment of groups. Freud, in his work *Group Psychology and the Analysis of the Ego*, also tried to explain the behavior of groups. He began by making reference to LeBon but found a stumbling block in the latter's accounting of the reasons for certain group behavior. Freud wrote,

> Group psychology is concerned with the individual as a member of a greater whole organized into a group at a particular time and for particular purposes. It is easy to regard the phenomena that appear under these special conditions as being expressions of a special instinct that is not further reducible, the social instinct ("herd instinct," or "group mind"), which does not come to light in any other situation. But we may perhaps venture to object that it seems difficult to attribute to the factor of number a significance so great as to make it capable by itself of arousing in our mental life a new instinct that is otherwise not brought into play.[4]

LeBon gave the impression that the curious transformation that takes place with individuals when they become a part of a crowd happened just because of the fact of numbers gathering. Freud could not accept this. LeBon did raise this question of numbers and added that there are predisposing conditions involved plus the fact of numbers.[5] Even with this qualification, LeBon's account still retained a quasi-mystical dimension that Freud did not want to admit.

In place of LeBon's explanation, Freud offered his in terms of the Oedipus theory. Freud reinterpreted group behavior in terms of object-cathexis and identification. Freud argued that what was influencing group behavior was the emotional tie to the leader and emotional ties among the members of a group because of the common tie to the leader. This may have accounted for some of the bonding mechanisms involved, but it did not adequately explain the singular behavior of individuals in groups that LeBon described such as the diminishing of intelligence, or the moral sense.

Ironically, although Freud disagreed with LeBon, there is a noticeable similarity in Freud's description of the unconscious and LeBon's view of the crowd. The following features apply to both:

Both are powerful agents and sources of power.
Both tend to behave in an infantile way.
Both tend to ignore morality.
Both respond to and relate through images and symbols.
Neither one entertains contradiction.
Both disregard time and place.
Both behave instinctively.
Both respond to the "magical" power of words.
Both tend to exaggerate and distort.
Both are highly suggestible.
Both tend to combine indiscriminately what normally is considered distinct.
Both tend to favor emotional-irrational modes as opposed to intellectual-logical ones.

In a sense, we can say that the crowd provides an external manifestation of the internal conditions of the unconscious. If there is any truth to this correspondence, then the methods of observation and analysis of one can be used to understand the other. The psychology of the unconscious and the psychology of crowds can inform each other. This is pure speculation and limited to the Freudian understanding of the unconscious.

When we consider Carl Jung, we are considering someone who, unlike Freud, was more in accord with the metaphysics accepted by LeBon. Jung would not have been threatened by a mystical analysis. Freud in principle rejected any such explanations. Jung made some comments regarding certain collectivities that reflect a LeBonian understanding of groups. Jung wrote, in a couple of places, the following:

> It is a notorious fact that the morality of society as a whole is in inverse ratio to its size; for the greater the aggregation of individuals, the more the individual factors are blotted out, and with them morality, which rests entirely on the moral sense of the individual and the freedom necessary for this.[6]

and,

> Any large company composed of wholly admirable persons has the morality and intelligence of an unwieldy, stupid, and violent animal. The bigger the organization, the more unavoidable is its immorality and blind stupidity.[7]

These are, to say the least, very strong statements. The overriding impression of groups one gets from these comments of Jung and those by LeBon is decidedly a negative one. LeBon did however mention briefly that crowds can be heroic, inspired, and idealistic. Outside of a few comments to that effect, he was mostly concerned with the negative features of crowds. Maybe history has recorded more instances of "bad" crowds than "good" crowds.

With LeBon, we have our first explicit example of the socio-cultural definition of the unconscious. It is a function of individuals coming together. It operates without the awareness of its participants, and it is some thing.

## THE RACIAL UNCONSCIOUS

We have already had an introduction to this idea of a racial unconscious in the earlier presentation of Gustave LeBon's ideas. The construct will also be discussed in reference to Carl Jung's construct of the collective unconscious in the section following this one. At this point though, we want to identify the racial unconscious as a construct in its own right. We also want to make the point that LeBon,

Freud, and Jung, although they differed on many issues, were in agreement in accepting the idea of a racial unconscious. Between Freud and Jung, it is Jung who is usually thought of as postulating the idea, and Freud as the one who was not receptive to it. Before we address this question, a word should be said about the idea of a racial unconscious in general.

The rationale for speculating on the existence of a racial unconscious is simple. It is largely an argument by analogy. Just as the individual has a personal history and memory, which are somehow recorded in one's being, so too with the race as a whole. Also, just as the physical body is the result of years of cumulative anatomical history, so too with the nonphysical side of the race. It too is the result of accumulating experiences. Somehow and somewhere, each person carries within oneself the physical and psychological history, not only of oneself but also of the group and race. The "somehow" and "somewhere" has been speculated to be the unconscious, both individual (personal unconscious) and racial. Just as the individual is considered a "whole," so too the larger collectivity in which one belongs can be considered an integral "whole." In this case, the whole (race) may be more than the mere sum of its parts (individuals).

Freud and Jung each used this argument by analogy. William A. White, in his article "Primitive Mentality and the Racial Unconscious," repeated that argument this way,

> That the psyche is necessarily as old as the body; it has therefore its comparative anatomy just like the body and it is a no more difficult matter to think in terms of its history through its different levels than it is to trace anatomical formations back through various types of related species to their origin.[8]

Another main reason for speculating on the existence of a racial unconscious was the failure, in psychotherapeutic practice, to explain certain psychic contents solely on the basis of the personal history of the patient. We already mentioned this point in our earlier presentation of Jung. We will encounter it again in the discussion of the collective unconscious. It is less known though that Freud also speculated about the racial unconscious. He once wrote,

Whence comes the necessity for these phantasies, and the material for them? There can be no doubt about the instinctual sources; but how is it to be explained that the same phantasies are always formed with the same content? I have an answer to this which I know will seem to you very daring. I believe that these "primal phantasies" are a phylogenetic possession. In them the individual . . . stretches out . . . to experiences of past ages.[9]

In another place, Freud commented that he fully agreed with Jung in recognizing the existence of a phylogenetic heritage, but considered it a methodological error to resort to the latter before the ontogenetic possibilities have been exhausted.[10]

Sigmund Freud and Carl Jung were much closer on this point of racial inheritance than is usually suspected. In fact, Steven Heyman devoted an article to make this point.[11] Notwithstanding the agreement between Freud and Jung on the question of racial memories, the idea was part of the minor considerations of Freud, whereas, for Jung, it formed a major part of his theory. It should be noted that both men were aware of the difficulties involved in assuming the inheritance of acquired characteristics. This may be the reason why Jung stopped writing about a physical mechanism of transition in his later writings.

## The Collective Unconscious

Carl Jung was the principal exponent of this construct. We present it here within the socio-cultural context because it refers to the unconscious of a human collectivity. As such, it seems to fit well with the definition of the unconscious in this approach. To a great extent this is true, but sometimes Jung wrote about the collective unconscious in such a way as to imply that it was before Humanity was and that it transcends Humanity. As such, it is not only or merely a function of peoples. One gets the impression that the collective unconscious is an independent entity orchestrating lives and events behind the scenes. This dimension of it would put its discussion within the transpersonal-spiritual approach and indeed it is present there. The point here is that Jung's construct of the collective unconscious will be treated as a borderline concept. It spans the boundary between the socio-cultural and the transpersonal-spiritual domain.

When Jung was introduced within the Psycho-Personal Approach, it was stated that he claimed to have found more in the unconscious than could be accounted for solely on the basis of the personal experiences of the patient. For this and other reasons, Jung distinguished between the personal unconscious and the collective unconscious. The latter is inherited, impersonal, universal, and shared by all people. A person is both an individual and Humanity. Jung wrote,

> Insofar as no man is born totally new, but continually repeats the stage of development last reached by the species, he contains unconsciously, as an "a priori" datum, the entire psychic structure developed both upwards and downwards by his ancestors in the course of the ages. [12]

June Singer made this the theme of her investigation, that is, that "fossil man," "archaic man," and "modern man" coexist in the depths of each person's psyche. Primordial consciousness has become, in time, primordial unconsciousness. "It is the psychological 'fossil man' who lives and breathes in every contemporary human being," [13] and it is the collective unconscious that unites them.

Another reason for postulating the existence of the collective unconscious is the similarity of myths and symbols among various peoples in the world. How to account for this? Jung was not the only one to speculate on this question. Some have argued that there was only one source and that, through travel and migrations, ideas were diffused from that source. Claude Levi-Strauss argued that similar brain structure is responsible for similar expressions. Others suggested that people, worldwide, face similar basic life experiences and so similar forms of expression is likely. Others choose to believe that God or some extraterrestrial Being gave us these symbols. For Jung, the answer was found in the collective unconscious.

There are two ways to visualize all that Carl Jung conveyed by this construct of the collective unconscious. One way can be called the "grand mirroring" argument, and the other the "layer cake" model. We will discuss first the former one. It has taken various forms within the Jungian corpus. Jung relied on it often. He believed in an *unus mundus* which expresses itself in two forms—external and internal. Just as there is an external, visible, substantial universe, there is a corresponding internal, invisible, substantial universe. As the individual psyche is composed of a conscious and unconscious aspect, so too the collective psyche is composed of a collective conscious and a collective unconscious. The latter is estimated to be 2,000,000 years old; the collective conscious about 5,000 years old. Consciousness, with the ego as its center, sits on the boundary between the two universes. Between the ego and the collective conscious operates the persona; between the ego and the collective unconscious is the self. Any external event has a corresponding internal manifestation. "As above so below" is the rule of thumb here. The grand mirroring goes on and on.

Jung contended that the collective unconscious worked to compensate for any imbalances in consciousness. This is so both on the individual and the collective level. This microcosm and macrocosm are constantly moving toward unity, balance, and harmony. Also, there is a teleological factor at work, guiding each toward some destiny.

Another expression of this grand mirroring involves Jung's use of the relationship between the individual and society. He wrote,

> We shall probably get nearest to the truth if we think of the conscious and personal psyche as resting upon the broad basis of an inherited and universal psychic disposition which is as such unconscious, and that our personal psyche bears the same relation to the collective psyche as the individual to society. [14]

also,

> Just as the individual is not merely a unique and separate being, but is also a social being, so the human psyche is not a self-contained and wholly individual phenomenon, but also a collective one. [15]

The final expression, that we will consider, of Jung's method of mirroring manifests itself in his account of the archetypes. He paralleled the phenomenon of archetypes with the phenomenon of instincts as a way of explaining the former. Jung relied heavily on this analogy. Everything that instincts mean to our physical life, archetypes mean to our psychic life and modes of understanding. Instincts are characteristically impersonal, universal, uniform, hereditary, dynamic, recurring, unlearned; they are regulating factors and are typical modes of actions. According to Jung, all these attributes apply equally well to archetypes, except that the latter operate within the medium of the psychical. Instincts and archetypes are the external and internal expressions of one ordering principle operating in the universe.

Now that we have a sense of Jung's vision of the collective unconscious on its broadest scale, we want to consider it as it relates to the socio-cultural context. This is where the layer cake model is appropriate to describe what Jung had in mind. It seems that Jung understood the psyche to be structured according to layers. There is not just one unconscious, but many, that interpenetrate one another. They represent systems within systems, and, the further down one goes, the more commonly shared and broader the base becomes. Ultimately the unique self reaches out and makes contact with the world. Between the personal and individual consciousness and the world are various levels of the collective unconscious. Each level is a function of the different collectivities from which a person emerges and in which one lives. It seems that every larger group one belongs to has a collective psyche with conscious and unconscious dimensions.

The idea of the collective unconscious is not an easy one to comprehend. Jung himself admitted that it was the most misunderstood of his ideas. It is not surprising that many Jungians who write about Jungian psychology include a chapter on the collective unconscious and on the archetypes hoping that they have made it clear. We will continue the discussion of the collective unconscious in the next major typological approach when we present the construct of the unconscious within the romantic tradition.

## Collective Preconscious

The focus here is on the ideas of Armando Morales. Morales in his article "The Collective Preconscious and Racism" was mainly concerned with individual and institutional forms of racism as they affect Mexican Americans. What we are concerned with is how he employed the construct of the collective preconscious and why it was significant for the problem of racism. Regarding the origin of the construct he wrote,

> The concept of the collective preconscious was developed from the works of Blumer, Lewes, Giddings, Durkheim, LeBon, Freud, Jung, and Moreno as a beginning concept for an understanding of some of the collective, social-psychological dynamics that might be found in white racism, a phenomenon that is apparently passed on from generation to generation. [16]

In this one sentence, Morales provided us with a quick reference list associated with such constructs as collective conscious, collective preconscious, and collective unconscious. Because Morales derived his ideas from a variety of sources, it is important to understand his own definition of the terms. He defined the key words this way:

> The term *collective* will be understood to mean the simultaneity, uniformity, or similarity of a response to a stimulus among many members of a group or society. [17]

> The term *preconscious* is preferable to unconscious because it refers to thoughts that are unconscious at a particular moment but are not repressed . . . not necessarily unacceptable . . . and capable of becoming conscious. [18]

> The term *collective* will be understood to mean the simultaneity, uniformity, or similarity of a response to a stimulus among many members of a group or society. [17]

Why was it so important for Morales to develop this particular concept? His primary concern was racism. He realized that racism goes on in an unintentional, disguised, and unconscious manner. He was looking for a way to understand the unconscious dimension of racism in a way that could hold somebody responsible and in a way that could bring about a change for the better. For these reasons he preferred the expression "preconscious" to the expression "unconscious" vis-à-vis the collective. The former word, he felt, had connotations that could serve his purposes better than the latter one. Why?

Preconscious is understood to mean that something is just below the level of awareness which, in turn, implies that it could easily become conscious. In reference to racism, this means that racism can be seen, not as rooted in some deep, inaccessible region, but in an accessible one. It can be more easily exposed, analyzed, and dealt with. Racism, in this sense, becomes something a society can do something about provided that some attention is given to its subtle manifestations. Racism cannot then be conceived of as something lodged deep within the society that cannot be reached or in such a way that the society is said to be involuntarily perpetrating it.

Morales felt that such concepts as collective unconscious, group mind, and racial unconscious are usually understood as being somehow inherited biologically. He commented,

> Their collective unconscious biological inheritance, however, assumes a vertical generational collective process rather than an unconscious, non-biological horizontal group inheritance.[20]

He wanted to draw out the distinction between the idea of inherited and acquired regarding the collective unconscious and, with that distinction, imply that racism is not just an inherited pattern from the past, but is something acquired now through the present psychosocial behaviors and processes of a society. In this way, someone can be held responsible; that is, not our ancestors, but the contemporary society. The present society practices racism and is responsible for its continuation.

With Morales we can see an interesting theoretical move being proposed in the conceptualization of the construct of the unconscious that is largely motivated by sociopolitical reasons. His example points out how theoretical terms and their redefinitions do have very practical consequences.

## Motion Pictures as Cultural Dreams

We are considering here the suggestion that motion pictures are an expression of the unconscious of a society. Individuals have dreams, but can a society be said to dream? We will present the ideas of three people who evidently believe that societies can have dreams. This question is discussed here because to answer yes to the above question is to implicitly accept a socio-cultural definition of the unconscious. The following three writers used the word "unconscious" and are assuming that a group, society, and culture have collectively held unconscious minds that find expression in motion pictures. The three will be presented and comments about them will be made after the presentations since the three can be responded to in a similar fashion.

The first example is Melvin Goldstein, who wrote "Film as a Cultural Mirror of the Unconscious of the Masses." Essentially, this article is a review of Paul Monaco's work: *Cinema and Society: France and Germany During the Twenties.* Goldstein used both the words "unconscious" and "subconscious," and used them as if they were synonymous. The point he made was that motion pictures express the unconscious wishes of peoples and help to release their fantasies. In the end, he asked a provocative question: "Are film-makers our new 'priests' of a new religion?"[21]

The second example is John W. Conner, who wrote "The Projected Image: The Unconscious and the Mass Media." Interestingly, the word "unconscious" is never again used in the article. Connor contended that motion pictures give symbolic expression to the underlying hopes, fears, and anxieties of the age.[22] He made basically the same point that Goldstein made except that Connor dealt with a different country and a different time—America in the 1960s and 1970s.

The third example is M. Sabini, who reviewed the religious images in the following motion pictures: *Star Wars, Close Encounters of the Third Kind,* and *Oh, God.* Sabini felt that these films can be treated like "dreams of a culture."[23] Sabini interpreted these "dreams" as portraying one's search for a spiritual connection and that each film reveals a different aspect of the ego-self relationship. Sabini was working with the Jungian understanding of these terms. Three films of the 1980s have come out as sequels to the ones just mentioned. They are: *The Empire Strikes Back, E.T.,* and *Oh, God II.* It would be interesting to have Sabini's sequel interpretation.

In general, all three examples are highly suggestive accounts. There is little theoretical discussion in any of them regarding the use of construct of the unconscious. It is simply assumed. Also, treating films and dreams as analogous phenomena is a limited enterprise. True, both work with symbols and images. But, whereas dreams are spontaneous events occurring in sleep, films are highly premeditated productions. Notwithstanding these comments, the point here is that these three examples represent a type of literature that uses the word "unconscious" and is using it according to a socio-cultural definition of the notion.

## Implicit Examples of the Socio-Cultural Type

### JOHN STEINBECK'S "PHALANX"

Clifford Lewis entitled his inquiry "John Steinbeck: Architect of the Unconscious." It is an interesting title indeed, for what is an "architect" of the unconscious? Lewis never explained his use of that expression. In any case, this work is one of a small number of studies that relate a construct of the unconscious and some literary figure or work. For our purposes, we will make use of Lewis' treatment of Steinbeck to present the latter's idea of "Phalanx."

It is Lewis' contention that Steinbeck's works "drive home the psychological theory that the unconscious was a more important factor in motivating people than economics and other external influences."[24] According to Lewis, Steinbeck sought to prove that the explanation for group behavior lies in the archaic experiences of a common unconscious.[25] Steinbeck believed that a group psyche-memory exists, which is the foundation of the unconscious, and that its ultimate base is in humanity's ancient marine experiences.[26] Along with these ideas, Steinbeck believed in inherited psychic patterns that are somehow imprinted in our being.[27] These preliminary comments prepare the stage to introduce the concept of "Phalanx."

Lewis, quoting Steinbeck, wrote,

> Now a man, while he is made of cells, which in turn are made of atoms and electrons and so forth, by no means has the natures of his parts or small units. So man is not the final unit. He also arranges himself into larger units, which I have called phalanx. And just as man's nature is not the nature of his cells, so the phalanx by no means has the nature of man.[28]

Lewis went on to explain that a phalanx is a group or a society with its own special psychological structure. The phalanx has its own memory stretching all the way back to humanity's supposedly marine life. When someone acts as a part of a phalanx, they lose their own nature in the nature of the phalanx. Steinbeck believed that two kinds of consciousness coexist in a person. One functions when the person is alone and another that assumes control when a group assembles.[29] As Lewis put it, "in short, the phalanx became a new psychological being for Steinbeck. This form of collective mentality would be the subject of his literature for fifteen years."[30]

Lewis made references to particular works of Steinbeck. Regarding *In Dubious Battle,* Lewis reported that the novel demonstrates Steinbeck's efforts to comprehend the psychological entity that is created by groups of people. There are three separate phalanxes in the novel.[31] In Steinbeck's "The Vigilante," which involves the lynching of a Negro, we have a case study that would illustrate a LeBonian analysis of crowd behavior. In fact there are distinct echoes of LeBonian ideas in Steinbeck's works. Reference the lynching story, Steinbeck did not believe that a desire for justice could explain the fanatic ritual of the hanging. According to Lewis, John Steinbeck implied that the real meaning of the ritual could be understood in terms of crowd magnetism, the symbiotic relationship resulting from an individual melting into the mob, and even some emotional mechanism such as that which responds to sexual intercourse.[32] In the lynching scene the central figure Mike loses himself temporarily in the mob only to resume his identity after withdrawing from the mob. It is interesting that Steinbeck intuited a sexual dimension to group behavior. Freudians would smile in agreement.

To conclude with the concept of the phalanx we have another example of the unconscious which illustrates the socio-cultural definition. Although the phalanx is not referred to explicitly as the unconscious, it is understood that the phalanx comes into being and operates without the awareness of any one of its constituents. This is why we refer to it as an implicit example. In some ways, the phalanx notion is similar to Carl Jung's construct of the collective unconscious, especially regarding the allusion to the group ancestral memory.

### THE INHERITED CONGLOMERATE

"Inherited Conglomerate" was an expression first used by Gilbert Murray in a lecture.[33] We learn of it through E. R. Dodds, who, in his book *The Greeks and the Irrational,* made use of the concept to sum up what he had written in the first five chapters of that book. Regarding the subject of religious beliefs, Dodds showed that there had been in the Greek culture prior to the Classical period a slow accumulation of various religious ideas. This had taken place over a long period of time and as a result of the successive religious movements that had occurred. That aggregate of beliefs, Dodds called, borrowing Murray's expression, the "Inherited Conglomerate." Dodds commented,

> The geological metaphor is apt, for religious growth is geological: its principle is, on the whole and with exceptions, *agglomeration,* not substitution. A new belief pattern very seldom effaces completely the pattern that was there before: either the old lives on as an element in the new—sometimes an unconfessed and half-conscious element or else the two persist side by side, logically incompatible, but contemporaneously accepted by different individuals or even by the same individual.[34]

If we expand the scope of what comprises the Inherited Conglomerate beyond just religious beliefs to include all beliefs, we can see the analogy to what Jung referred to as the "Collective Psyche." This latter construct is composed of a collective conscious and a collective unconscious. Also, without drawing analogies, we can say that any culture has its official and spoken system of beliefs and rules as well as those which are unspoken, unofficial, and many times followed without awareness. We then have the options to speculate that such a system of ideas exists, as such, outside, above, or around the individuals involved, or that it exists in some mini-aturized form within each individual, or that it doesn't exist at all as any thing, but is simply a referrent to name the sum of various behavior patterns of a culture. Within a socio-cultural approach, the Inherited Conglomerate can be considered an expression of the first option although it need not be.

Dodds never used the expression "the unconscious" in a noun form. It could be argued though that had he entitled his book "The Greeks and the Unconscious," very little regarding the substance of the book would be lost. Indeed, the unconscious has always been considered, by certain traditions of thought about the topic, the source of irrational and nonrational phenomena. Also, the way Dodds described the relationship of ideas in the Conglomerate, that is, as logically incompatible but co-existing, is a description of one of the features of the unconscious. It is stated that the unconscious knows no contradiction. Finally, the "unconfessed and half-conscious elements" of the Conglomerate could be considered the unconscious aspect of it. For these reasons, we can consider the construct of the Inherited Conglomerate as an implicit example of the socio-cultural definition of the unconscious.

## THE FAMILY

Here we will present the ideas of Carl Whitaker and Augustus Napier, who are family psychotherapists. They proposed the idea that a family including father, mother, and children can be looked at also as "the Family," implying that we're talking about an entity of sorts. The theoretical foundation for this type of thinking is the systems theory principle that the whole is more than the sum of its parts. A family is more than just the sum of its members. This "more" that it is is indicated by the designation "Family."

The practical foundation for this theory comes from the practice of family psychotherapy. Whitaker and Napier have observed that, along with the individuals that compose a family, there seems to be another member present but invisible. This "something" behaves as if it has a life of its own. They did not observe it in the sense that they saw anything, but it was more of a speculation that they developed in order to make sense of some of the phenomena that occurred within the context of family therapy. They found that this Family usually has an ambivalent attitude toward therapy. They noticed how a family can unconsciously collude and conspire among its members for various goals, roles, and functions. Many times the family's unconscious intentions are in direct opposition to the conscious, spoken intentions of the family members.

Each family has a working, usually unspoken and unreflected ideology about what a family is and how it is to operate. It is shaped by many factors and changes due to many variables. Whitaker and Napier contend that "It" (Family) is there. A therapist is always dealing with the individuals of a family and the Family. The latter is the hidden, silent member of a family.

Here are three quotes from Whitaker and Napier that summarize their thinking:

> Scientists began to think of the family in a new way. Rather than look at it as a collection of individuals, they began to view the family as having almost the same kind of organized integrity that the biological organism has. The family functioned as an entity, as a "whole" with its own structure, rules, and goals.[35]

> Every family is a miniature society, a social order with its own rules, structure, leadership, language, style of living, zeitgeist.[36]

> The family members move in precise planetary orbits around one another. They are a world, a solar system, a small universe of experience.[37]

In sum, we have with the idea of the Family another example of the socio-cultural definition of the unconscious. In this case, it emerges as function of the individuals making up a family. This Family evolves and operates with or without the awareness of it of the individuals involved. In this sense, the Family represents the unconscious of a particular family.

## Rejections of the Socio-Cultural Definition

### EDWARD SAPIR (AND OTAKAR MACHOTKA)

Edward Sapir does believe that many of our behavior patterns are acquired unconsciously, that we may be unable to articulate why we do certain things, and that we may not know the significance of some of our actions, but he does not believe in a social mind as a construct to help understand these things. Sapir wrote,

> We may seem to be guilty of a paradox when we speak of the unconscious in reference to social activity. . . . It may be argued that society has no more of an unconscious than it has hands or legs.[38]

What he expressed seems logical enough, but it is not completely true to experience, which sometimes shows us that a society can act as if it did have hands and legs. We do say, for example, that one society is outrunning another society, or that one society is grabbing everything from another. These remarks may be examples of personification, but they are not meaningless or paradoxes.

Sapir is fundamentally against what he would regard as mystifying notions put forth to account for certain social behavior. He is content to account for such behavior as being the learned result of many unconscious social patterns that make up any human environment. He is right to a great extent.

Sapir also wrote,

> patterns of social behavior are not necessarily discovered by simple observation, though they may be adhered to with tyrannical consistency in the

actual conduct of life. If we can show that normal human beings . . . are reacting in accordance with deep-seated cultural patterns, and if, further, we can show that these patterns are not so much known as felt, not so much capable of conscious description as of naive practice, then we have the right to speak of the "unconscious patterning of behavior in society." The unconscious nature of this patterning consists not in some mysterious function of a racial or social mind reflected in the minds of the individual members of society, but merely in a typical unawareness on the part of the individual of outlines and demarcations and significances of conduct which he is all the time implicitly following. Jung's "racial unconscious" is neither an intelligible nor a necessary concept. It introduces more difficulties than it solves.[39]

What Sapir just expressed is probably an adequate summary of the opinion of many sociologists. This is a good point to introduce Otakar Machotka, another sociologist.

Otakar Machotka wrote a book entitled *The Unconscious in Social Relations*. Despite the noun form usage of the word "unconscious," his ideas are more in line with Edward Sapir's than with our socio-cultural definition of the unconscious. In a sense, it can be said that Machotka did precisely what Sapir suggested in the quote above when he remarked "if we can show that normal human beings . . . are reacting in accordance with deep-seated cultural patterns. . ." That is what Machotka did in his book. He spelled out the thousand and one unconscious processes and patternings that go on in a society. He described the many subtle ways we learn, communicate, understand one another, respond, and perform certain activities without much deliberate, direct attention to what we are doing or what is happening.[40]

The title of Otakar Machotka's book is misleading. It should have been entitled "The Unconscious Processes in Social Relations." The word "unconscious" was used in a careless way. Why the noun form, rather than the adjectival or adverbial form, was used is a mystery because it is completely superfluous, misleading, and unnecessary in the approach and the substance of the book.

What we have, in sum, is an explicit rejection of the socio-cultural definition of the unconscious by Sapir, and an implicit one by Machotka. Sapir thought that social behavior could be accounted for without appealing to a construct of a social mind. LeBon and Jung, of course, would disagree. What can be said here though is that if we remember the system theory principle and the example of the family therapists, we see a case where it was helpful to hypothesize a social mind (in this case referred to as Family) to account for certain behavior in the smaller society of the family. It may be that such concepts as social mind, group mind, and so forth, although not completely intelligible or strictly necessary, represent an attempt to do justice to some experiences involving groups. This is particularly so when a group behaves as if it were one collective entity.

## TWO MARXIST CRITICS

Two rejections of the Freudian unconscious are discussed here, but the comments can be considered to apply to the socio-cultural type of unconscious as well as many of the psycho-personal types. In general, any construct of the unconscious that implies that it is an entity is rejected. We present these criticisms here in the socio-cultural approach because Marxist psychologists put an exclusive accent on the external-social dimension and relegate the internal-psychic factors to a very minor position.

The first critic is Albert Starr. He described the idea of the unconscious as a middle-class intellectual expression, an imperialistic notion used to obscure the class basis of the drive to war, a fiction that robs human consciousness of its importance, a tool used by the ruling class to maintain power by attacking the credibility of the rational human mind which could expose the irrationalities of capitalism, and a ploy to divert attention away from the social nature of problems by pointing to some mysterious force working beyond anyone's control. He maintained that the negative attributes of the unconscious, such as primitive, chaotic, antisocial, and so forth, are really reflections of the capitalist society, and that Freud's penis envy theory is a cover-up of the real reason for the psychological disturbances of women—their inferior, exploited position in society.[41]

Besides the alleged capitalist foundation for the construct of the unconscious, Starr had other reasons why the concept should be rejected. First, the construct involves the acceptance of an idealist philosophical position giving too much priority to the value of ideas. Second, the construct involves focusing on the past and reducing the present events to past ones. This point of view tends to deny that anything new can happen. Marxists sense that, with a Freudian understanding of the unconscious, there would be an end to history and humanity would be condemned to repetition. Third, it involves an emphasis on a subjective as opposed to an objective approach to change. All these reasons trespass the sacred theoretical grounds of dialectical-materialism and the whole Marxist-Leninist enterprise.

Albert Starr went on to state that if unconscious mental forces do not exist, then the problem of unawareness ought to be analyzed in a different way. When a person's understanding of themselves is inaccurate it is because they may be unaware of the inaccuracy of some of their ideas, or they may be unaware of the consequences of some idea or act, or they may be unaware of the significance of certain activity, or they may be unaware of the significance of others' behavior, or they may be unaware of the full importance of an idea.[42] In short, Starr is referring to a certain ignorance (unawareness) on the part of a person.

The next critic is Francis H. Bartlett, who responded to and continued the line of argument we have just presented. Bartlett was not as extreme in his expressions as Starr was. In some ways, Bartlett's argument is similar to Edward Sapir's in that both men focused on the social aspect of a person's life as being determinative. Also, both realized that a person may not fully understand the nature of the matrix they emerge out of and live in. In fact, Bartlett contended that a person may have a "false consciousness" of the objective reality even though they are a reflection of that reality. But Sapir did not share the political agenda that Bartlett worked with.

In the following quote, Bartlett refers to Sigmund Freud. It is to the point and presents a fascinating reversal of perception. Bartlett wrote,

> Freudians, being idealists, interpret the patient's unawareness or distorted awareness as evidence of the "Unconscious." They are able to do this particularly when a person's spontaneous responses do not coincide with his own better judgment and where he therefore feels that these

responses are governed by alien forces. It is this phenomenon which is conceptualized by Freudians as the "Unconscious" or "Id." Actually the person's spontaneous responses are governed by forces quite the opposite of alien. They are governed by his actual social being, the operation of which he is largely unaware of and does not understand.[43]

For Bartlett there is no mystery; the source of neurotic symptoms is in the patient's social practice and nowhere else.

One is tempted to smile at the ideas of these two men for appearing to only represent Marxist propaganda, but their approach does force us to take a closer look at the situation and to determine to what extent they could be right. Interestingly, both Freudians and Marxists pride themselves for being "unmaskers" of what is false. The Marxists, in this case, may have uncovered the class basis of the Freudian enterprise.

## Conclusion

We have come a long way from discussing dogs in harnesses and other features of laboratory experimentation. We have also come a long way from dealing with childhood experiences, personal feelings, and the motivation of one individual. We are referring here to the Bio-Physical and Psycho-Personal approaches. In the Socio-Cultural Approach, we are involved in a discussion of the unconscious on a collective level, that is, related to many individuals at one time and when they are grouped together.

If in the Psycho-Personal Approach we asked why a person does what one does, in the Socio-Cultural Approach we ask why does a person, in a group, behave as one does? Generally, we presented two points of view. One view, accepting the socio-cultural definition of the unconscious, contends that individuals, when they group themselves, form something more than the sum of their numbers and that this something acts as the invisible, controlling member of the group. We identified the various explicit and implicit examples of the social forms that the unconscious can assume.

The other point of view rejects the socio-cultural definition of the unconscious and argues that a person's behavior in a group can be accounted for by investigating the subtle, unofficial, and unnoticed patterns of responses between members of a group. In short, one approach is to talk about the unconscious created by a group and working in the group, and the other approach is to talk about the many unconscious processes happening in a group. The former makes use of the noun form of the word "unconscious," and the latter approach uses the adjectival form.

Our discussion does not prove or disprove that any unconscious exists under group conditions. We have reported, though, on those who believe it does exist as well as on those who do not. Today, except for the Jungians and a few scattered voices, one hears very little talk of a collective mind, conscious or unconscious. There may be an occasional metaphorical allusion to such, but rarely is it conceived of in a realist sense. We saw though, with Armando Morales and the two family therapists, two relatively current examples of some who have entertained a socio-cultural definition of the unconscious and have applied it toward the analysis of social problems and in psychotherapy. It is possible that the psychotherapists have observed something that can be relevant to the greater society. After all, a family is a miniature society. We are referring here specifically to systems theory. This construct of systems may be the middle position between the two opposing ones that we set up earlier. Systems theory allows us to speak about systems rather than entities and allows us to investigate patterns of behavior within a system such as a group, society, and so forth.

# Notes

1. Gustave LeBon, *The Crowd* (London: Ernest Benn Limited, 1930), pp. 177–82.

2. Ibid., p. 26.

3. Ibid., p. 31.

4. Sigmund Freud, *Group Psychology and the Analysis of the Ego* (New York: Liveright Publishing Corporation, 1951), p. 3.

5. LeBon, *The Crowd*, p. 26.

6. Carl Jung, "Phenomena Resulting from the Assimilation of the Uncon-

scious," in *The Collected Works of Carl Jung,* vol. 7 (Princeton: Princeton University Press, 1966), p. 153.

7. Ibid., p. 153.

8. William A. White, "Primitive Mentality and the Racial Unconscious," *American Journal of Psychiatry* 4 (1924–1925), p. 670.

9. Sigmund Freud, *A General Introduction to Psychoanalysis* (New York: Pocket Books, 1971), p. 324.

10. Sigmund Freud, *The Complete Psychological Works of Sigmund Freud,* ed. J. Strachey, vol. 17: "An Infantile Neurosis" (London: The Hogarth Press, 1955), p. 97.

11. Steven R. Heyman, "Freud and the Concept of Inherited Racial Memories," *The Psychoanalytic Review* 64, no. 3 (1977), pp. 461–64.

12. Jung, *Collected Works,* vol. 9, part 1: "Conscious, Unconscious, and Individuation," p. 279.

13. June Singer, "Culture and the Collective Unconscious," unpublished doctoral dissertation, Northwestern University, 1968, p. 29.

14. Jung, *Collected Works,* vol. 7: "Phenomena Resulting from the Assimilation of the Unconscious," p. 147.

15. Ibid., p. 147.

16. Armando Morales, "The Collective Preconscious and Racism," *Social Casework* 52, no. 5 (1971), p. 293.

17. Ibid., p. 287.

18. Ibid., p. 289.

19. Ibid., p. 290.

20. Ibid., p. 289.

21. Melvin Goldstein, "Film as a Cultural Mirror of the Unconscious of the Masses," *Journal of Psychohistory* 5, no. 3 (Winter 1978), p. 450.

22. John W. Connor, "Projected Image: The Unconscious and the Mass Media," *Journal of Psychoanalytic Anthropology* 3, no. 4 (Fall 1980), p. 375.

23. M. Sabini, "Review," *Quadrant* (Winter 1978), p. 105.

24. Clifford Lewis, "John Steinbeck: Architect of the Unconscious," unpublished doctoral dissertation, University of Texas at Austin, 1972, p. v.

25. Ibid., p. 181.

26. Ibid., p. 14.

27. Ibid., p. 182.

28. Ibid., p. 25.

29. Ibid., p. 112.

30. Ibid., p. 27.

31. Ibid., p. 127.

32. Ibid., p. 112.

33. Gilbert Murray, *Greek Studies* (Oxford: Clarendon Press, 1946), pp. 66ff.

34. E. R. Dodds, *The Greeks and the Irrational* (Berkeley, California: University of California Press, 1951), p. 179.

35. Carl Whitaker and Augustus Napier, *The Family Crucible* (New York: Harper & Row, 1978), p. 47.

36. Ibid., p. 79.

37. Ibid., p. 80.

38. Edward Sapir, "The Unconscious Patterning of Behavior in Society," in *The Unconscious, A symposium,* ed. C. M. Child (New York: Alfred A. Knopf, 1927), p. 114.

39. Ibid., p. 121.

40. Otakar Machotka, *The Unconscious In Social Relations* (New York: Philosophical Library, 1964).

41. Albert Starr, "Psychoanalysis and the Fiction of the Unconscious," *Science and Society* 15 (1951), pp. 129ff.

42. Ibid., p. 141.

43. Francis H. Bartlett, "Marxism and the Psychoanalytic Theory of the Unconscious," *Science and Society* 16 (1952), pp. 49–50.

Chapter V

# Transpersonal-Spiritual Approach

## Introduction

The expression "Transpersonal-Spiritual" is the fourth major generic term of this typological investigation. It represents that aggregate of literature and ideas that discusses the unconscious in terms of a transpersonal entity or as the medium to contact transpersonal entities. In either case, the noun form of the word "unconscious" is used almost unanimously in the literature of this type. Sometimes the word is capitalized as "Unconscious" and sometimes it reads "The Unconscious."

The neologisms that have appeared within this framework include:

Extra-Terrestrial Unconscious      Trans-Individual Unconscious
Synchronistic Unconscious          Teleological Unconscious
Absolute Unconscious               Super-Consciousness
Collective Unconscious             Objective Psyche
Higher Unconscious                 Cosmic Unconscious

The adjectives used in the above list already convey the sense of the bigger-than-life dimension of the unconscious that will be discussed in this approach.

## The Unconscious in the Romantic Tradition

When we talk about the Romantic tradition, we are referring to the Philosophy of Nature school of thought. Vitalistic biology is one

115

of the derivatives of this tradition. There is no mistaking the trans-personal nature of the construct of the unconscious that has emerged from the writings of representatives of this movement. Those we will present include Carl Carus, Eduard von Hartmann, Gustave Geley, George Groddeck, Carl Jung, and D. H. Lawrence. The one feature that unites these thinkers is their "grand vision" of what the unconscious is and is able to do.

Henri Ellenberger, in commenting about the Romantics, wrote,

> [These persons] considered Nature a gigantic collective being in which the stars, earth, everything were parts, bound together by a "sympathy," and undergoing a collective organic development . . . individual human unconscious mind was but a ramification of the unconscious soul of the world. [1]

"Soul of the World" is probably the key expression to describe the vision of The Unconscious held by this school of thought. The former expression comes from the title of a book by Friedrich Schelling *On the Soul of the World* (1798). With it, he inaugurated the Romantic philosophy and psychology school of thought. The idea of a World-Soul can be traced down and back through the neo-Platonic tradition. Carus, Hartmann, Geley, and others acknowledged their debt to that tradition. We will now present some specific ideas these men had about the Unconscious.

## CARL GUSTAVE CARUS

One can quickly grasp the sense of Carl Gustave Carus' orientation by reading this remark of his:

> After seeing the world as an aspect and revelation of the divine, who would not be deeply convinced of the necessity for an inner intelligence in all natural life. [2]

We may debate his conditional premise, but not his conclusion. Natural life, Mother Nature, does reveal a most sophisticated intelligence, order, and design. What to call that intelligence or who or what to assign it to is not as self-evident. Many have and many still assign it to God. In fact, this is the essence of one of the five classical proofs for the existence of God that was propounded by Thomas Aquinas. Carus assigned this intelligence to the Unconscious.

Here is a summarized list of Carus' description of the Unconscious:

It is the source of the conscious life of the soul from which it emerges.

It possesses a certainty and wisdom with which it goes its precise way.

It never rests, never stops, and never gets tired.

The vital functions of the realm of the unconscious need no practice or study, all is done and achieved easily and immediately.

It never forgets anything.

It is the primordial source of life and its life is instinctively merged with the life of the universe.

It is promethean (goal orientated) and epimethean (has an unconscious memory of the past).

It never gets sick and works to overcome any illness suffered by the person.

Carus distinguished three aspects of the Unconscious, namely, the Absolute Unconscious, Partial Absolute Unconscious, and the Relative Unconscious. The first refers to the region of the life of the soul that is inaccessible to consciousness. The second governs all the forming, sustaining, and re-creating processes of the human organism. It exerts an indirect influence on our emotional life. The third aspect is that region of the conscious life that may for a time become unconscious but returns to consciousness again and again. This can include feelings, thoughts, and perceptions.

## EDUARD VON HARTMANN

Eduard von Hartmann acknowledged his debt to both Friedrich Schelling and Carl Carus. In reference to the former he wrote that "we find in Schelling the conception of the Unconscious in its full purity, clearness, and depth."[3] He mentioned that it was Gottfried Leibniz who first inspired him to the study of the Unconscious. He also stated that the theme of his book was mainly "the elevation of Hegel's unconscious Philosophy of the Unconscious into a conscious one."[4]

Hartmann gave the following involved definition of the Unconscious,

> I designate the united unconscious will and unconscious idea "The Unconscious." Since, however, this unity only rests upon the identity of the unconsciously willing and unconsciously thinking subject, the expression "the Unconscious" denotes also this identical subject of the unconscious psychical function—a something in the main unknown . . . When we view the world as a whole, the expression "the Unconscious" acquires the force not only of an abstraction from all unconscious individual functions and subjects, but also of a collective, comprehending the foregoing both extensively and intensively . . . Lastly, all unconscious operations spring from one same subject, which has only its phenomenal revelation in the several individuals, so that "the Unconscious" signifies this One Absolute subject.[5]

Here we see that the Unconscious refers, not only to a condition of unity, but also to two levels of subjectivity—the individual and the collective. The three aspects are interpenetrating and inseparable.

Hartmann accepted the attributes that Carus assigned to the Unconscious and extended the list of descriptions to include the following:

> The Unconscious forms and preserves the organism, repairs its inner and outer injuries, appropriately guides its movements.

> The Unconscious supplies very being in its instinct with what it needs for self-preservation.

> The Unconscious preserves the species through sexual and maternal love, ennobles it through selection in sexual love . . . conducts the race to perfection.

It does not err.

It needs not time for reflection, but instantaneously grasps the result at the same moment in which it thinks the whole logical process that produces the result.

The Unconscious often guides people in their actions by hints and feelings.

It furthers the conscious process of thought by its inspiration in small as in great matters and in mysticism guides mankind to the presentiment of higher, supersensible unities.

It makes us happy through the feeling for the beautiful and artistic production.[6]

When we combine Carus' and Hartmann's lists, we have a composite sketch of a very awesome Being. Some of the features that they assigned to the Unconscious others have used to describe the attributes of God, and to what can be referred to as Mother Nature. In fact, many phenomena that we today would casually refer to as Mother Nature's work, the Romantics would take to be a proof for the Unconscious. For example, Carus and Hartmann would interpret the healing of a broken bone as evidence of the mysterious powers of the unconscious psyche. This type of approach and reasoning permeates their writings.

Hartmann, like Carus, also distinguished three levels of the Unconscious. He called them Absolute Unconscious, the Physiological Unconscious, and the Psychological Unconscious. Essentially, these three correspond to the three distinctions that Carus made.

We can derive another perspective of our subject by something Victor White once stated. He commented that the Unconscious of Carus and Hartmann is similar to the "All-Unity" of Idealist philosophy, the "Substance" of Spinoza, the "Absolute Ego" of Fichte, the "Absolute Subject-Object" of Schelling, the "Absolute Idea" of Plato and Hegel, and the "Will" of Schopenhauer.[7]

## GUSTAVE GELEY

Gustave Geley wrote a book called *From the Unconscious to the Conscious*. In the opening pages he remarked that this work was the logical sequel to his other book—*The Subconscious Being*. He added that the purpose of *From the Unconscious to the Conscious* was to "bridge the chasm that Schopenhauer leaves between the Unconscious and the Conscious, but instead of leading to pessimism . . . leads to optimism."[8]

Arthur Schopenhauer was the second major expounder, next to Schelling, of the Philosophy of Nature school. Geley is an inheritor of this tradition. He too shared the vision of the Unconscious as some grand mysterious force that creates, directs, and sustains all life forms. He found materialistic-oriented sciences inadequate to account for many phenomena. In fact, it seems that the other purpose of his book was to argue against the evolutionary theory. He offered an explanation in terms of what he called the "dynamo-psychism" which orchestrates natural life. He considered this to be a spiritual force or being that somehow is responsible for natural and seemingly supernatural phenomena.

In general, Geley repeated the approach and many of the ideas of Carus and Hartmann. There is an unmistakable harmony of thought and vision among Carus, Hartmann, and Geley. It is as if they were three expressions of one spirit.

## GEORGE GRODDECK

Strictly speaking, George Groddeck cannot be considered to have followed the tradition of Carus, Hartmann, and Geley. Even so, his understanding of what he called "It" resembles some of the ways the latter three understood the Unconscious. For this reason Groddeck is presented here.

Groddeck, in giving us synonyms for the It, acknowledged another tradition. He wrote that the It can be considered synonymous with the Hippocratic *physis,* Galen's "creative power of nature," Georg Stahl's "unknown intelligence," and Jan van Helmont's "ruler, the Archaeus which resides in the body."[9] Even though

Groddeck did not explicitly acknowledge the tradition of Carl Carus, Eduard von Hartmann, and Gustav Geley, he did write about the It in some ways very similar to the way the Romantics wrote about the unconscious. For this reason he is presented in this particular section.

Interestingly there is a place in Hartmann's *The Philosophy of the Unconscious* that bears remarkable similarity to what Groddeck referred to as "It." In one place, Hartmann quoted Wilhelm Wundt, who wrote that "this unconscious soul, like a benevolent stranger, works and makes provisions for our benefits, pouring only the fruits into our laps."[10] Hartmann then commented that "we are vividly reminded of Wundt's unconscious soul, which works for us like another being, when Bastian begins his 'Contributions to Comparative Psychology' with the words 'That it is not we who think, but that it thinks in us, is clear to him who is wont to pay attention to the internal processes. This 'it' lies . . . in the Unconscious."[11]

Groddeck himself stated that he borrowed the term "It" from Friedrich Nietzsche in order to formulate his (Groddeck's) theory of the It. Groddeck commented,

> I believe that whatever happens in or through man, from the moment of conception to the moment of death, even what he reasons out for himself and does of his own free will as we say, everything is directed by this unknown It.[12]

In another place, Groddeck referred to the It as the Unknown Self.

There is an interesting relationship, regarding the construct "It," between Groddeck and Freud. Freud once wrote,

> I am speaking of Groddeck, who is never tired of insisting that what we call our ego behaves essentially passively in life, and that, as he expresses it, we are "lived" by unknown and uncontrollable forces. . . . following Groddeck in calling the other part of the mind, into which this entity extends (ego) and which behaves as though it were Unconscious, the "id."[13]

Groddeck wrote this in reference to Freud,

The Freudian "Unconscious" . . . is not what I mean by the "It": it comprises only what was conscious at one time or at one stage of development, but has since been lost to consciousness. Together with the conscious mind it makes up the psyche . . . the Unconscious is a part of the psyche, the psyche is a part of the It.[14]

In other words, for Groddeck the It is the foundation of both the conscious and unconscious aspects of the psyche.

We get a sense from these quotations of what Groddeck was alluding to. He considered the It to be a secret thing, the workings of which nobody knows.

### CARL JUNG

When we last discussed Carl Jung's ideas, in the Socio-Cultural Approach, it was said that his construct of the collective unconscious would be treated as a borderline concept. It relates to the previous approach because some aspects of it are a function of people (the race). However, Jung also wrote about the collective unconscious in ways that conveyed a sense that it was independent of the race. With this nuance, the collective unconscious (here maybe more appropriately referred to as the Objective Psyche) is understood to precede, sustain, and transcend the race. This rendition of it puts its discussion within the transpersonal-spiritual dimension. Interestingly, Jung himself denied this at one point; that is, he maintained that the collective unconscious was not to be thought of as a self-subsistent entity.[15] Even Walter Shelburne, who, in his investigation attempted to downplay the point that Jung was talking about a subsistent entity with an ontological status and locus outside of the human.[16] Even so, as will soon become evident, Jung's one sentence denial is no real deterrent to the effect of many sentences which affirm a sense of the collective unconscious as being a self-subsistent entity. Also, Jung was an inheritor of the Romantic tradition, and he himself acknowledged his connection to Carus and Hartmann, both of whom believed and articulated a vision of the Unconscious as a subsistent entity. Why Jung tried to deny this is not clear, but such inconsistencies in the Jungian corpus are not uncommon.

When Jung reviewed the complex theory, he referred to complexes as the *"living units* of the unconscious."[17] (Emphasis added here and in the following quotations.) Later, when he expanded his theory beyond the complex to include archetypes, he referred to archetypal material in this way: "These transpersonal contents are not just inert or dead matter that can be annexed at will, rather they are *living entities.*"[18] In another place, Jung distinquished himself from Freud in this way,

> In this respect I go several steps further than Freud. For me the unconscious is not just a receptacle for all unclean spirits and other odious legacies from the dead past. . . . It is in very truth the *eternally living, creative, germinal* layer in each of us.[19]

In still another place Jung wrote,

> What one sees happening in the world is not just a "shadowy vestige of activities that were once conscious," but the expression of a *living psychic condition* that still exists and always will exist.[20]

From these few quotes, we have an image of the unconscious as something living. Not only is it living, but it has a life of its own. Jung wrote,

> Dealing with these contents [of the unconscious] . . . brought home to me the crucial insight that there are things in the psyche which I do not produce, but produce themselves and have their own life.[21]

Also, he wrote that "experience shows that the objective psyche is autonomous in the highest degree,"[22] and that "we are a psychic process which we do not control, or only partly direct."[23]

In sum, the collective unconscious is alive, has a life of its own, and partly controls every individual life. This is not all. The collective unconscious operates with a teleological factor. It has a groundplan, a destiny to fulfill for each person and for the race, and we have little to say about it. Ann Ulanov repeated this point once by quoting Jung himself. Jung commented that "one really has only two choices—

willingly to respond to one's destiny, or unwillingly to be dragged there through neurosis or psychosis."[24] Along these same lines is the following account by Magda Arnold who wrote an encyclopedia entry about Jung's Analytical Psychology. Arnold wrote,

> Jung's is not a Christian world view; it is far closer to that of Carus and von Hartmann, for whom the supra-individual unconscious psyche, absolute and eternal, is the source of consciousness, "the Divine within us." Jung's process of individuation is really the reclamation of matter by the divine unconscious, and man has only the choice of going along or being dragged along.[25]

From this series of comments we can see that Jung's denial that the collective unconscious is a subsistent entity is a weak one, and that it probably represents the view of the early Jung. He made this denial around 1922. By way of concluding this discussion of Jung, we can refer to something he wrote in his latter years. He once speculated:

> I have, therefore even hazarded the postulate that the phenomenon of archetypal configurations . . . may be found . . . upon an only partially psychic and possibly altogether different form of being . . . we have good reason to suppose that behind this veil there exists the uncomprehended absolute object which affects and influences us.[26]

### D. H. LAWRENCE

D. H. Lawrence's understanding of the unconscious has certain recognizable features in common with the vision of it so far presented. His connection, in particular, to vitalistic biology has been noted.[27] Also, some of his statements about the unconscious are virtually indistinguishable from remarks made by Carus or von Hartmann. For example, Lawrence wrote,

> [The unconscious] is that active spontaneity which rouses in each individual organism at the moment of fusion of the parent nuclei, and which, in polarized connection with the external universe, gradually

evolves or elaborates its own individual psyche and corpus, bringing both mind and body forth from itself. Thus it would seem that the term "unconscious" is only another word for life. But life is a general force, whereas the unconscious is essentially single and unique in each individual organism; it is the active, self-evolving soul bringing forth its own incarnation and self-manifestation.[28]

Here he has given us a description of the unconscious within a personal context. On a transpersonal level, he also remarked that the laws of the universe are the fixed habits of what he called the "living unconscious."

One particular feature of the Laurentian unconscious is its relationship to blood. David Kleinbard, in his thesis on Lawrence, commented that Lawrence's unconscious is a blood consciousness, and very close to the Old Testament expression, "The life of the flesh is in the blood" (Lev. 17:11).[29]

An ironical footnote on Lawrence is that, although he considered Freud "the great enemy spokesman, engaged in the analysis but not the advocacy of the Unconscious";[30] Lawrence is considered the "most capable dramatist of the oedipal theme in twentieth century literature."[31] Lawrence carried out a private war against what Freud represented, that is, rationalism and intellectualism. Lawrence believed that Freud was wrong about the unconscious. It was not a cellar or shadow of the mind as Freud made it out to be but the true unconscious is the spontaneous life-motive in every organism.[32]

With Lawrence, we conclude this presentation of the construct of the unconscious within the Romantic tradition. The individual expressions have been varied, but the impression regarding the unconscious is virtually the same, that is, it is a mysterious, awesome, all-influencing Being.

## Realms of the Unconscious

Here we are dealing with a variation of the transpersonal-spiritual definition of the unconscious. The unconscious in this context is not so much understood to be a substantive entity but a means or a medium through which one relates to transpersonal beings or dimensions. Four theorists will be considered who subdivided the unconscious by mapping its area in rather detailed ways. It is appropriate here to speak about realms rather than entities. Jung could be considered the modern-day prototype for this method of mapping. Before him, Carus and Hartmann also conceived the unconscious to be layered from the very personal level to the ultimate transpersonal level. Likewise, our four theorists expounded a view of the unconscious as being layered, but in more detail and more layers than did Jung, Carus, or Hartmann. The four include Stanislav Grof, Kenneth Ring, Kenneth Wilber, and Roberto Assagioli. We will outline their respective map of the unconscious and then make some general comments about their approach to the topic.

The four theorists did not neglect the bio-physical or psycho-personal dimensions, but subsumed them within their broader conceptualization of what the unconscious includes. We present them here because they entertained the transpersonal dimension.

### STANISLAV GROF

Stanislav Grof delineated four levels of the unconscious. He did it with the help of LSD, of which he said, "LSD can be used as a kind of 'inner radar' that scans the unconscious."[33] He was suggesting that LSD could be another royal road to the unconscious. He explored four types of LSD experiences that he contended correspond to areas of what he referred to as the human unconscious. The four are: aesthetic experience, psychodynamic experience, perinatal experience, and transpersonal experience.

The *aesthetic* experiences occur in the initial stages of the LSD experience. They involve sight and sound (psychedelic) phenomena, and are chiefly the function of sensory organs. The *psychodynamic* experiences encompass all that relates to the Freudian unconscious. Grof accepted it uncritically. The *perinatal* experiences are referred to as Rankian, and here Grof acknowledges and accepts Rank's work. Grof wrote,

Perinatal experiences are a manifestation of a deep level of the unconscious that is clearly beyond the reach of classical Freudian techniques . . . and explanations. . . . Perinatal experiences represent a
very important intersection between individual psychology and transpersonal psychology.[34]

Concerning *transpersonal* experiences, Grof said that they were
experiences involving an expansion or extension of consciousness
beyond the usual ego boundaries and beyond the limitations of time
and space.[35] These experiences are supposed to occur after the subject
has worked through and integrated the material on the psychodynamic and perinatal level. What Grof included within this category makes up an awesome list of experiences. They include: embryonal
and fetal experiences; ancestral, racial, evolutionary, and past-incarnation experiences; precognition, clairvoyance, time travels, identi-
fications with other persons, plants, and animals; oneness with all
creation, consciousness of inorganic matter, planetary and extra-
planetary consciousness; cellular consciousness, archetypal experiences, encounters with deities, consciousness of Universal Mind,
experience of the Supercosmic and Metacosmic Void, etc.[36] In short,
he included every conceivable paranormal, parapsychological, and
mystical type of experience.

Grof focused on early birth and prebirth experiences and made
some powerful claims for LSD. Before we end this particular section,
we should mention someone who also worked with LSD and birth
experiences but did not speculate beyond the personal level. Frank
Lake made use of LSD for its alleged ability to revive early birth
experiences. He claimed to have confirmed Rank's point about the
significance of the birth trauma. He certainly did not confirm Grof's
ideas. Lake confined himself to what we have called the psycho-
personal dimension of a person's life. He did not speculate beyond
that level as did Grof. He did though use a definition of the unconscious but one very different from Grof's. Lake stated:

The unconscious is the aggregate of the forces and contents of the mind
which are not ordinarily available to conscious awareness, or to voluntary

recall. The activities of the unconscious mind are not open to direct, conscious scrutiny, but have dynamic effects on conscious mental life and behavior. At times, "preconscious," or "subconscious" are properly used of areas of mental life on the edge of awareness, recoverable without resistance. The deep unconscious is often, in psychoanalysis, equated with the id.[37]

Lake's understanding of the levels of the unconscious is more closely related to Freud's than to anyone within this section dealing with realms of the unconscious. Lake belongs properly in the Psycho-Personal Approach. We have presented him here to compare and contrast his work with that of Grof's on the matters of LSD and the birth trauma.

## KENNETH RING

With Kenneth Ring we have more of same type of speculations that Grof indulged in, but without LSD and with even more distinctions regarding realms of the unconscious. Ring mapped out eight regions of what he called "inner space." The eight regions are (my paraphrased summary):

The *Preconscious,* which is similar to the Freudian "preconscious" and Assagioli's "middle unconscious."

The *Psychodynamic Unconscious,* which is similar to the Freudian unconscious.

The *Ontogenetic Unconscious,* which relates to Grof's and Rank's work with perinatal experiences. Ring, like Grof, considered this a transitional zone between the personal and the transpersonal dimensions.

The *Trans-Individual Unconscious,* which is the first of the transpersonal realms of consciousness. This includes ancestral, past-incarnation, racial, and archetypal experiences.

The *Phylogenetic Unconscious,* in which we encounter our own evolutionary development from the very beginning.

The *Extraterrestrial Unconscious,* which includes out of the body experiences wherein one encounters entities and guides, and one travels to other parts of the universe. It makes possible mediumistic phenomena, telepathy and clairvoyance, spirit possession, and automatic writing.

The *Superconscious,* wherein we reach "the edge of consciousness" where experiences become increasingly ineffable, including ecstasy and merging with Universal Mind.

The *Void,* which is a state beyond any content whatever.[38]

Ring commented that this map of consciousness refers to the "voyage that all of us are destined at some time in our lives to take, for ultimately each one of us will travel to the farther regions of inner space."[39]

Two years after he proposed the map just cited, he revised it. He made it more graphic by using a circle from whose center all the various types of experiences listed previously were shown to radiate. It indicated a progression from one experience to another, from the personal to the ultimate transpersonal level. The center of the circle he called the "psychic transfer point," and corresponded to the psychodynamic unconscious. He wrote,

> It is here that awareness can either continue its "downward" drift into deeper levels of body-based memories and experiences or it can take a "horizontal" turn into realms of experience which are independent of the body.[40]

### KENNETH WILBER

Kenneth Wilber put forth a theory outlining five dimensions of the unconscious. He remarked that "the psyche—like the cosmos at large—is many-layered (pluridimensional), composed of successively higher-ordered wholes and integrations."[41] We will now briefly describe the five types.

The *Ground Unconscious* includes what Wilber called "deep structures," which exist as potentials ready to emerge. Deep structures are the defining forms of a level as opposed to "surface structures" which are simply a particular manifestation of a deep structure.

The *Archaic Unconscious* consists of instincts and archetypes, which are closely related to what Sigmund Freud called "archaic heritage" and Carl Jung named "phylogenetic heritage."

The *Submergent-Unconscious* includes what Carl Jung called the "personal unconscious" and Sigmund Freud termed the "repressed unconscious."

The *Embedded Unconscious* is that which is unconsciously identified with and used to perceive the world. We "see" by it, but cannot "see" it. This type has some resemblance to Freud's construct of Superego.

The *Emergent-Unconscious* is that which has the potential for transpersonal experiences.[42]

### ROBERTO ASSAGIOLI

Roberto Assagioli distinguished four aspects regarding the unconscious. The four are (my paraphrased summary):

The *Lower Unconscious,* which includes physiological processes, fundamental drives, complexes, dreams and imaginations of an inferior kind, uncontrolled parapsychological processes, and various pathological manifestations, such as phobias, obsessions, delusions, and compulsive urges.

The *Middle Unconscious,* which is the area where our experiences are assimilated, where imaginative activities are elaborated before arising into consciousness, and in general is easily accessible to waking consciousness.

The *Higher Unconscious* or *Superconscious,* the source of higher intuitions and inspirations, the source of higher feelings, of genius, and of states of ecstasy, contemplation, and illumination.

The *Collective Unconscious,* which Assagioli commented corresponds to Jung's notion of "collective unconscious."[43]

Assagioli acknowledged the closeness between his system and

Jung's, but he did see them as distinct. Assagioli contended that, regarding the collective unconscious, Jung disregarded its many distinctive features and spoke of it *en bloc*. For Assagioli the collective unconscious is a "vast world stretching from the biological to the spiritual level, in which, therefore, distinctions of origin, nature, quality, and value must be made."[44] He also warned against conceiving of the unconscious as an entity. Carus and Jung, among others, also issued this warning but to little avail.

To conclude, the four theorists, between them, have coined about twenty neologisms regarding the unconscious. Many are similar and refer to basically the same things, but they have been given different names. The immediate question that has to be raised is that if one unconscious or any unconscious is still a debated issue, what service to this controversy does this blatant multiplication of unconsciouses offer? It does a disservice, because distinctions prematurely offered can only promote more confusion surrounding the topic.

There would have been fewer problems had theorists confined themselves to only distinguishing types of experiences and forgo, at least for now, the added task of assigning a new type of unconscious to each type of experience. The neologisms are actually superfluous to their discussions of experiences. The experiences themselves, many of them, are still subject to so much speculation and debate that there is no need to further complicate the issues by dragging in or conjuring up unconsciouses to account for those experiences.

## The Unconscious Conceived To Be a Power

In this section we want to identify and discuss what is probably the most popular understanding of the unconscious. By "popular" we mean that understanding of the unconscious that is conveyed in certain paperback literature, which appeals to the person's desire to be more, have more, and do more. These are the typical "How to . . ." books; for example, how to become rich, how to heal, how to develop one's psychic powers, how to be more creative, etc. It is not uncommon to find a chapter on the subconscious in this type of book. We should note here that, in this type of literature, the expression "subconscious" is more prevalent than the expression "unconscious." In general, the overall image one gets of the subconscious is that it is some mysterious thing that possesses amazing powers or can induce powers to work. One has only to learn how to tap it, tune in to it, or awaken it in order to make things happen. This image fits the transpersonal-spiritual definition of the unconscious because it refers to some "outside" agency or a means to contact some "outside" agency or power.

One example of this type is the one proposed by Napoleon Hill. Regarding the subconscious mind he wrote,

> The subconscious mind consists of a field of consciousness which receives, classifies, records, stores impulses which can later be recalled . . . it draws upon the forces of Infinite Intelligence to transmute desire and ideas into their physical reality . . . it is the connecting link.[45]

Hill also referred to it as the connecting medium between one individual's subconscious mind and another individual's subconscious mind. This makes telepathy and the healing of others possible. The subconscious mind is also the means to send prayers and the means to receive answers and inspirations. The subconscious is never idle, it cannot be entirely controlled, but it can be programed to work for us if we know how to work it. Hill's particular program involves thirteen steps. Autosuggestion is the key factor mediating between the conscious and the subconscious. He promised great things if one believes and follows his instructions.

There is very little attempt to discuss the theoretical foundations of his principles except to say that "nature has so built man that he has absolute control over the material which reaches his subconscious mind."[46] Rather than a theoretical foundation, Hill argued from what he considered a practical foundation, that is, it just works this way, if you don't believe it, try it.

Another example is Charles Bristol's book *The Magic of Believing*. The cover of the book reads: "A remarkable book that shows how you can turn your desires into realities by using the powerful forces of your subconscious mind."[47] This is how the subconscious is described:

> It is a repository of spontaneous impressions of men and nature, and a memory vault in which are kept the records of facts and experiences that are sent down to it from time to time by the conscious mind for safekeeping and future use . . . is also a powerhouse of energy with which the individual can be charged, thus enabling him to recover his strength and courage, and also his faith in himself . . . it is beyond space and time . . . is a powerful sending and receiving station with a universal hookup whereby it can communicate with the physical, mental, psychic, spiritual worlds, past, present, and future . . . it is a distinct entity closely allied to the physical body, but also operates independently of the body.[48]

The three primary functions of the subconscious are: 1) to maintain and preserve the well-being of the body; 2) in times of emergency it springs into action and takes command to save the life of the person; and 3) it is operative in telepathy, clairvoyance, and psychokinesis and can be summoned for help in problem-solving and to achieve goals.[49]

Finally, Bristol made this curious statement about the subconscious: "It must be trusted and believed in, patiently waited for, obeyed unconditionally even if inspired to do something irrational or seemingly meaningless."[50]

Another example, this time in the area of healing, comes from the ideas of Agnes Sanford. In her work on spiritual healing, she confidently stated that "the inner control center (the subconscious mind) is part of the spiritual body, the eternal Being. It acts under orders from God himself until one sends into it a contrary command and throws it into confusion."[51] In her book she outlines a method of healing that makes use of the belief in the existence of the subconscious mind and its connection to cosmic forces.

This next example is not from a book, but appeared in a magazine as an advertisement. It is an appeal made by an esoteric society known as The Rosicrucians. It reads:

YOUR  OTHER  SELVES . . . AWAKEN  THE  PSYCHIC  YOU
. . . There is more to you than you suspect. Self goes far deeper than
*surface consciousness.* Man is not fully *conscious*—that is, using the whole
potential of his awareness. . . . The occasional hunch, and the intuitive
flash are attributes of the psychic, *the real you,* awaiting fuller expression.
The use of these *levels of consciousness,* which are at your command, is but
the application of natural law. Creative imagination, reception of the
unspoken thoughts of others, the ability to clearly comprehend and
master circumstances are the result of the awakening *psychic self.*[52]

Cultic and occult magazines, in general, are full of this type of
appeal.

Coincidentally, as this page was being typed, over the radio came
an advertisement about the subconscious mind. It was sponsored by
the advocates of Scientology. It made reference to research on the
subconscious mind that had supposedly isolated something in it
called "the reactive mind." The contention was that this reactive
mind is the root cause of a person's unhappiness and misfortunes in
life. In order to overcome the influence of this reactive mind, one was
to send for L. Ron Hubbard's book *Dianetics* and learn how.

We could mention many other examples. Here we will simply list
some books that are similar in spirit to those already mentioned in
this section. These books include: Frederick Pierce, *Our Unconscious
Mind and How to Use It;* Erna Grabe, *The Sub-Conscious Speaks;* The-
odore Foote, *The Source of Power;* Joseph Murphy, *The Power of Your
Subconscious Mind;* Raymond Barker, *The Power of Decision;* Charles
Clark, *Brain-Storming;* Shaw Desmond, *Personality and Power;* Jean
Guitton, *Make Your Mind Work For You;* John Williams, *The Wisdom
of the Subconscious* and *The Knack of Using Your Subconscious Mind.* We
could also include the article by Michael Crampton entitled "Answers From the Unconscious." All of the preceding examples make
use of some variation of the theme of this section, namely, that the
subconscious is a power that can be used.

In Crampton's short article,[53] we find something usually missing
in all the other examples cited so far—warnings. Crampton offered
some precautions regarding the dealing with the unconscious. Literature of the type we are discussing tends to encourage an attitude of
naive trust and childlike (sometimes childish) playfulness in regard to

the mysterious powers within. There is little hint at the possible negative consequences of playing with the subconscious mind. Crampton though warned that one can bite off more than one can chew. Also, he cautioned to be careful about who or what one may contact for an answer or help through the unconscious. Not all voices are from God, and not all spirits are friendly. The medieval mind was careful to distinguish the work of demons and that of angels. Today, we need that same kind of discretion and discernment regarding the potential help or danger of being open to the subconscious (or unconscious) mind. The literature that we have presented seems to have neglected this in its excitement over the fantastic powers of the subconscious.

These next comments are made in an attempt to provide some background to the various examples cited in this section. Most of the preceding examples traffic in the phenomenon and practice of suggestion and autosuggestion. These are an integral part of most methods suggested for using the subconscious mind. Suggestion and autosuggestion, as such, can be traced to a book by that title written by Charles Baudouin. In it, he defined the subconscious in this way:

The subconscious (the term does not mean an "inferior or subordinate consciousness," but a "hidden consciousness," a consciousness that lies at a lower level than the familiar consciousness of everyday life) is comparable, to use Pierre Janet's simile, to the deeper geological strata. The subconscious is a storehouse of the memories that have lapsed from the ordinary consciousness, of wishes and sentiments that have been repressed, of the impressions of a distant past. But it is far from being inert, for it contains in addition the subsoil waters which are unceasingly at work; it contains the suggestions which will well up into the open after their hidden passage. This is all imagery, but it serves, better than pure abstractions, to convey some notion of the complex reality we have learned to recognize in the subconscious.[54]

Baudouin's main preoccupation was hypnotic phenomena. He contended that autosuggestion was the main factor involved and that the subconscious was the key operative area involved, and it follows the law of reversed effect. Because it obeyed this law, the subconscious could be programed to work for us.

In Baudouin's ideas we have one clue to a possible tie between the type of understanding of the unconscious we have presented in this section and the tradition of medical psychology. Baudouin followed the tradition of Franz Mesmer, Jean Charcot, Émile Coué, and others. This is the tradition of the use of hypnotism. It is difficult to determine how much it influenced the rise of the popularized understanding of the subconscious. Outside of this tradition, one can only guess that another major tradition contributory to the type we have presented is the tradition of various esoteric and mystical groups. There are also some traces of the Romantic tradition detectable here.

In sum, we see that for some the unconscious (subconscious) is a promised land of hope and power. One has only to believe, trust that it will work, follow some formula, and then wait for the fantastic results. As we said earlier, there is very little theoretical discussion in this area. The rationale is along the lines of, "We don't understand it fully but it works."

All mystifying language aside, without exception this type of literature is built upon some form of suggestion and autosuggestion. It appears that the human being is so equipped that suggestion and autosuggestion, in combination with other elements such as faith, desire, and so forth, can produce extraordinary results. It is possible that this type of literature represents the unofficial experimentation with one's ability to create and do. We are referring to a person's mindpower over psychic and physical matters. To use the biblical expression, we are referring to the "faith that can move mountains." The efficacy of suggestion and autosuggestion is directly a function of a faith-factor, that is, how much a person believes and trusts that it will work. This faith power has never been measured and just beginning to be officially studied in some areas of parapsychological research.

## The Unconscious as the Contact with the Spiritual World

Virtually everyone mentioned in the Transpersonal-Spiritual Approach shares a common belief that through the unconscious a person is connected with the spiritual world. This world can include God, gods, angels, ancestors, and other transpersonal entities, beings, or powers. We will highlight this nuance of the construct of the unconscious by presenting the ideas of those who made this the major feature of their treatment of the construct. The theorists include Frederick Myers, Ernest White, O. Hobart Mowrer, Morton Kelsey, Victor Frankl, and Norman Goldman.

## FREDERICK MYERS

Frederick Myers, the nineteenth century psychologist, at various times used such expressions as: "unconscious self," "transcendental self," and "subliminal self." It is for this last expression that he is best known. Myers believed that a person possesses a soul which survives bodily death.[55] For our purposes here, we can cite the following remarks by William James, who at one time reviewed the ideas of Myers regarding the subliminal self. James remarked:

> From its intercourse with this spiritual world the subliminal self of each of us may draw strength and communicate it to the supraliminal life. The "energizing of life" seems, in fact, to be one of its functions. The reparativeness of sleep, the curative effects of self-suggestion, the "up-rushing" inspiration of genius, the regenerative influence of prayer and of religious self-surrender, the strength of belief which mystical experiences give, are all ascribed by Myers to the 'dynamogeny" of the spiritual world, upon which we are enabled to make drafts of power by virtue of our connection with our subliminal.[56]

James himself was not as convinced as Myers was about the spiritual world. James admitted though that, if there be higher spiritual agencies that can influence our life, it is possible that that influence is facilitated by the subconscious aspect of the personality.[57]

There is no need to go further with Frederick Myers' ideas except to note that he contended that a person is in contact with a spiritual world through the agency of the subliminal self.

## ERNEST WHITE

For Ernest White, the unconscious represented the setting in which the sacraments work, where spiritual rebirth begins, and where the Holy Spirit moves. It is also portrayed as the medium of prayers.

He used all three forms of the word "unconscious." As adverb, he said that God's work of molding the soul takes place within us unconsciously. As adjective, he said that spiritual regeneration occurs on the unconscious level. He wrote that "unseen spiritual forces are at work operating upon the minds of men, influencing them beneath the level of consciousness."[58] As a noun, he asked if salvation was possible for the subconscious? Also, he asked, "to what extent, if any, new birth affected the unconscious?"[59] He used the words "subconscious" and "unconscious" synonymously. His answer to his questions was that salvation is for the whole person, that it begins in the depths of one's heart (the unconscious) and eventually works its transforming power in all aspects of the person's life.

Ernest White's book *Christian Life and the Unconscious* is more about Christian life than the topic of the unconscious. There is no doubt though that he is referring to the subtle and hidden life of the Spirit within a person, and merely referred occasionally to the construct of the unconscious as the secular expression for the setting or condition of that hidden life.

## O. HOBART MOWRER

In the following discussion of Mowrer's ideas it is best to state early the identity equation that he presumed. For Mowrer, the unconscious is equal to conscience. One of the nuances of the latter concept is that it is the vehicle for the "Voice of God" to influence the person. The essence of Mowrer's argument is that each person has a conscience, which, when one acts against it, it sets into motion reactions which manifest themselves as anxiety and/or other symptoms. The person should then confess their breach of conscience, restore their sin, and thereby quiet their conscience so that it does not bother them anymore.

Mowrer performed an interesting reversal of the Freudian line of thinking about anxiety. He contended that anxiety does not come from evil acts people would perform if they dared, but from acts people have committed but wished they had not.[60] Mowrer invoked the names of William Stekel, Anton Boisen, and Havelock Ellis to support his contention that much of people's problems are derived from their unreleased consciences, their unconfessed sins, or their active defiance of the urgings of their consciences.

To illustrate how the unconscious (as conscience) works, he gave the following example:

> A child can operate in either of two ways: (1) of his own free will and wish, or (b) under parental compulsion. By acting "like a big boy (or girl)," that is to say, maturely and responsibly, the child enjoys many privileges and feels and indeed is "free." But if the child "forgets" or ignores what his parents have tried to teach him, they have to reassert their authority, with an ensuing loss of freedom and self-direction on the part of the child.[61]

Mowrer then went on to say that in like manner so it is for an adult's conscience, freedom, and problem if they violate their conscience. He then performed another reversal. The task was not to make the unconscious conscious, The unconscious, via the disturbances of conscience, is too much in evidence (too conscious already). The objective is to get it to subside, relax, retreat; and this can only be done when the ego has restored itself vis-à-vis conscience.[62]

Mowrer invoked some examples from the Old Testament to support his ideas. He wrote,

> If I understand the stories of Job, Nebuchadnezzar, and other Old Testament characters, there is no intimation that psychopathology necessarily involves repression: surely the very core of the problem is that God has spoken, expressed himself, touched the individual in question . . . the question is why God and conscience have smitten us and what we can do about it. . . . This is not to say, of course, that the now afflicted individual may not have previously repressed conscience and "denied God."[63]

This last quote leads us to present Mowrer's third major reversal of Freudian thinking. Mowrer contended that, whereas the Freudian model presents a picture of the ego and superego opposed to the id, it is now time to also see that the id and the ego can join forces against the superego.[64]

Mowrer, in general, wanted to restore the position of conscience within the mental health question, to deter the flight from conscience and guilt that he felt the Freudian system seemed to promote, and to maintain that the sinful model sometimes is more appropriate than the sick model regarding the psychic disturbances of an individual. Mowrer should not have equated (confused) the constructs unconscious and conscience. If he meant conscience, he should have stayed with the word and not try to translate one problematic expression (conscience) for another more problematic one (the unconscious).

## Morton Kelsey

It is an old and persistent belief that God communicates to people through their dreams. Kelsey is a modern-day advocate of this idea. He wrote,

> We consider the dream as a practical method of coming to know the reality of the spiritual world and the Christ who is victor there. . . . Once one knows this reality, it makes very little difference what name he gives to it. Call it the "unconscious" or the "spiritual world," the "objective psyche" or "heaven and hell," the "collective unconscious" or the "realms of gods and demons," or even "alam al-methal"—these are all merely names to describe what man finds as he listens to the reality that comes through the depth of himself.[65]

The key point, according to Kelsey, is the fact that God is in an intimate relationship with the psyche. He blamed Karl Barth, Rudolf Bultmann, and Dietrich Bonhoeffer for contending that a person has no direct and immediate contact with any nonphysical or supernatural realm. According to Kelsey, the dream is the proof that a person has direct contact with that realm. He felt that theologians should incorporate this fact into their systems.[66]

Along the same lines as Kelsey's is the book by John Sanford—

*Dreams: God's Forgotten Language.* Both of them considered dreams to be the vehicle of God's communications to people, and the unconscious as the common denominator for the interaction.

## VICTOR FRANKL

Frankl, in his book *The Unconscious God* used these expressions: "instinctual unconscious," "spiritual unconscious," and "the transcendent unconscious." The first is akin to the Freudian unconscious in the sense that it is the source of the sexual and aggressive impulses. This is contrasted to the spiritual unconscious that Frankl considered to be the source of spiritual impulses. The point he wanted to make by distinguishing these opposite types was to say that just as sexual and aggressive drives can undergo suppression and repression, so too can the spiritual impulses suffer these forms of denial. The end result of either type of denial is suffering for the person.

It is with his construct of the transcendent unconscious that Frankl relates to our discussion. The transcendent unconscious is the expression of a person's relatedness to transcendence on an unconscious level. According to Frankl, there is an inherent relationship between the immanent self and a transcendent thou. This is the source of the spiritual impulses.

Frankl was not very clear in his references to the three forms of unconscious. It is hard to determine if in fact he meant three because the spiritual and transcendent unconsciouses appear to be the same. In any case, according to him a person is related to God via the unconscious.

## NORMAN GOLDMAN

We want to present some of the ideas of Norman Goldman because they represent one point in the interface between Jewish theology and the psychology of the unconscious, and they are related to our discussion of a person's connection with the spiritual dimension.

Goldman admitted that in rabbinic literature there is no explicit reference to the unconscious as such, but that there are concepts that relate or can be related to it. One key concept is the idea of

"Shekinah" which means the Divine Presence in the world and in a person's life. Goldman wrote that "the rabbinic view of the 'Shekinah' is most appropriately translated into the contemporary idea of the 'collective unconscious' which contains the residual memories of one's cultural past. In rabbinic theology, the 'Shekinah' as the unconscious recalls and relives the encounter between God and man which is historic and contemporary, social, and intrapsychic."[67]

Goldman's ideas represent one contribution toward the apologetical efforts between psychology and religion. The question of Jewish theology and the construct of the unconscious is more involved than what is mentioned here. Here we are only focusing on one aspect, namely, the connection between the divine and the human.

When we look over the material that we have just presented, we notice two key points. First, there are those who believe that a person has a direct connection with the spiritual dimension. Second, some have spoken about that connection in terms of the unconscious. We are not questioning the first point. It is not our primary concern. But when we examine the second point closely, we find that the construct of the unconscious is really superfluous and even misleading in the contexts that it is used. By presenting the following chart we can summarize this section and make our point.

Myers:    subliminal world _____(Unc)_____ the person
Mowrer:   conscience _____(Unc)_____ the person
White:    hidden life of Holy Spirit _____(Unc)_____ the person
Kelsey:   God _____(Unc)_____ the person
Frankl:   spiritual impulses _____(Unc)_____ the person
Goldman:  Divine Presence _____(Unc)_____ the person

Essentially each theorist has simply and arbitrarily assumed and inserted something referred to as "the unconscious" between the person and something else. This gap-filling method is somehow supposed to add to our knowledge. The fact is, though, that the unconscious itself is not really explained. It merely functions as a X-factor. Why use the expression at all? To talk about spiritual impulses, conscience, and so forth, is problematic enough. We do not need to compound the difficulties by importing other problematic terms. Before the expression "the unconscious" was coined, the word "soul" was used to fill in the gap. We may try to change the names, but the questions and problems remain unchanged. We need new understanding, not new terms.

## Conclusion

When we concluded the Socio-Cultural Approach, we said that, with that approach, we had come a long way from discussing physiological psychology and childhood experiences. What can be said about where we have traveled when we conclude the Transpersonal-Spiritual Approach?

The sense of the distance traveled is made even more dramatic if we forget, for a moment, the Psycho-Personal and Socio-Cultural approaches. There is a wide gap between the Bio-Physical and the Transpersonal-Spiritual approaches. In the former we were involved exclusively with very limited areas of interest such as conditioning, automatic behavior, and so forth. In the latter approach we discussed topics of cosmic proportions. In the first three approaches, we were confined to studying phenomena related to things of this world. In this fourth approach, we were speculating about things possibly related to other worlds and other dimensions.

Despite the blatant and gaping disparity of subject-matter, one word unites them all—"unconscious." We may tolerate the use of one word to cover two relatively similar things, but it seems that the word "unconscious" (noun form) is stretched out of proportion when we try to use it to cover such diverse phenomena within both the Bio-Physical and the Transpersonal-Spiritual approaches. This is partly the reason why we contended earlier that, within the Bio-Physical Approach, the word "unconscious" is confused with other phenomena which can be articulated in more descriptive terms. The word "unconscious" doesn't belong in the Bio-Physical Approach.

What about the Transpersonal-Spiritual Approach, how does the word "unconscious" (noun form) function and does it belong here? In this approach, the word "unconscious" is used extensively in the noun form, usually implying that a thing or place is being referred to. In the Romantic tradition the construct is given even more significance by the designation "The Unconscious." There is no doubt here of the cosmic proportions of this awesome, impersonal, and mysterious Being or mode of Being. In the other areas of this approach, we saw the unconscious in less gigantic proportions, but still as some thing. We saw it portrayed as a miracle worker of sorts with powers just waiting to be used. We saw it imagined as regions or realms of the mind, with each realm providing a variety of experiences. Finally, we saw it conceived of as a medium that provides the connection between the natural and the supernatural. When one considers the now famous blessing of the 1970s movie *Star Wars,* that is, "May the Force be with you," it is this type of unconscious that comes to mind.

Now we ask whether the construct of the unconscious is legitimate and necessary in the Transpersonal-Spiritual Approach? Given the problematic nature of many of the experiences alluded to in this approach, the construct of the unconscious is at least as legitimate as any construct that is offered to account for the seemingly unexplainability of these experiences. Of course, those who do not believe in these experiences as reported, can reduce them to bio-physical and psycho-personal factors. This can even be done in terms of a construct of the unconscious. Sigmund Freud is the prime example of this reductive analytic. These reductionistic interpretations may satisfy the disbelief of the skeptics, but they do not do justice, and even offend, the faith of those who do believe in these experiences. These latter people try to find meaning in these experiences by hypothesizing something responsible for them, such as, soul, spirit, spirits, and so forth. For those not prone to use theological terms, the construct of the unconscious is employed as an explanation. It must be pointed out, though, that the construct of the unconscious functions as an X-factor that is not itself really explained, but at best only described. In sum, as an X-factor the construct of the unconscious is legitimate.

The construct of the unconscious may be legitimate, but is it the most appropriate one for explaining behavior? In other words, is the construct of the unconscious a necessary one for accounting for phenomena alluded to in this approach. At this point we say no, and looking back over the material covered in the Transpersonal-Spiritual Approach we can see why.

Within the Romantic tradition the construct of the unconscious has been assigned to phenomena others could and have attributed to the agency of God or Nature (Mother Nature). The construct of the unconscious is not a necessary one in this context; others are available.

In discussing the possibility of realms of the unconscious, we say that such distinctions are prematurely offered because the reality of one or any unconscious is still an unsettled question. Until and if it is settled, we can speak of experiences and phenomena without assuming realms of the unconscious to account for such things.

When we consider the construct of the unconscious as one representing a power, we can make a similar comment as that made in the previous paragraph. We can speak of a person's potential and capabilities without having to necessarily assign a special agent for these things. We still do not know fully what or who a human being is and is capable of doing. Each new power or ability does not warrant the creation of some special agency to account for it.

Finally, in discussing the suggestion that the unconscious be considered a connecting medium between a person and the spiritual world, we saw that it was an arbitrary construct assumed to function in the gap between the person and some spiritual dimension. Again, as we said in the previous two paragraphs, we can speak about spiritual influences without assigning special agents or places in the person that are responsible for them.

In sum, the construct of the unconscious in the Transpersonal-Spiritual Approach is legitimate but not necessary, that is, not the only option open to us to explain behavior. It apparently satisfies for some the need to assign a special causality in the face of seemingly unaccountable experiences, but it leaves others unsatisfied because the construct itself is as problematic as the experiences it is called in to account for. It should be pointed out that this is a judgment regarding the use of the construct of the unconscious as an explanatory one vis-à-vis certain transpersonal-spiritual events, and not a judgment regarding whether or not these events, and so forth, are genuine. These experiences, events, and phenomena are already problematic enough without importing or conjuring up more difficult terms to discuss, describe, or explain them.

# Notes

1. Henri Ellenberger, "The Unconscious Before Freud," *Bulletin of the Menninger Clinic* 21, no. 3 (1957), pp. 5–6.

2. Carl Gustave Carus, *Psyche* (New York: Spring Publications, 1970), p. 55. Originally written in 1846.

3. Eduard von Hartmann, *The Philosophy of the Unconscious* (London: Routledge & Kegan Paul, 1950), p. 24.

4. Ibid., p. 28.

5. Ibid., pp. 4–5.

6. Ibid., pp. 38–39.

7. Victor White, *God and the Unconscious* (London: The Harvill Press, 1952), p. 31.

8. Gustave Geley, *From the Unconscious to the Conscious* (New York: Harper & Brothers Publishers, 1920), p. x.

9. George Groddeck, *Exploring the Unconscious* (New York: Funk & Wagnalls Co., 1933), p. 8.

10. Hartmann, *The Philosophy of the Unconscious,* p. 40.

11. Ibid., p. 41.

12. Groddeck, *Exploring the Unconscious,* p. 210.

13. Freud, *The Standard Edition,* vol. 19, "The Ego and the Id," p. 23.

14. Groddeck, *Exploring the Unconscious,* p. 213.

15. Jung, *Collected Works,* vol. 15, "On the Relation of Analytical Psychology to Poetry," paragraph 126.

16. Walter Shelburne, "C. G. Jung's Theory of the Collective Unconscious: A Rational Reconstruction," unpublished doctoral dissertation, University of Florida, 1976, p. 89.

17. Jung, *Collected Works,* vol. 8, "A Review of the Complex Theory," p. 100.

18. Jung, *Collected Works,* vol. 7, "Phenomena Resulting from the Assimilation of the Unconscious," p. 145.

19. Jung, *Collected Works,* vol. 4, "Introduction to Kranefeldt's 'Secret Ways of the Mind,'" p. 330.

20. Jung, *Collected Works,* vol. 9, part 1, "Conscious, Unconscious, and Individuation," p. 280.

21. Carl Jung, *Memories, Dreams, Reflections* (New York: Vintage Books, 1961), p. 183.

22. Jung, *Collected Works,* vol. 12, "Introduction to Psychology and Alchemy," p. 51.

23. Jung, *Memories, Dreams, Reflections,* p. 4.

24. Ann Ulanov, "God and Depth Psychology," in *God In Contemporary Thought,* ed, S. Matczak (New York: Learned Publications, Inc., 1977), p. 949.

25. Magda Arnold, "Analytical Psychology," *International Encyclopedia of the Social Sciences,* vol. 1, ed, D. Sills (New York: MacMillan and the Free Press, 1968), p. 280.

26. Jung, *Memories, Dreams, Reflections,* p. 351.

27. Sidney Jordon, "D. H. Lawrence's Concept of the Unconscious and Existential Thinking," *Review of Existential Psychology and Psychiatry* 5, no. 1 (1965), p. 36.

28. D. H. Lawrence, *Psychoanalysis and the Unconscious and Fantasia of the Unconscious* (New York: Viking Press, 1960), p. 42.

29. David Kleinbard, "The Invisible Man made Visible, Representation of the Unconscious in the Writing of Lawrence," unpublished doctoral dissertation, Yale University, 1968, p. 482.

30. Philip Rieff, Introduction to *Psychoanalysis and the Unconscious and Fantasia of the Unconscious,* D. H. Lawrence (New York: Viking Press, 1960), p. xxiii.

31. Jordon, "Lawrences's Concept of the Unconscious," p. 34.

32. Lawrence, *Psychoanalysis and the Unconscious,* pp. 9, 13.

33. Stanislav Grof, *Realms of the Human Unconscious* (New York: Viking Press, 1975), p. 216.

34. Ibid., pp. 98–99.

35. Ibid., p. 155.

36. Ibid., pp. 156–57.

37. Frank Lake, *Clinical Theology* (London: Darton Longman & Todd, 1966), p. 1195.

38. Kenneth Ring, "A Transpersonal View of Consciousness: A Mapping of Farther Regions of Inner Space," *Journal of Transpersonal Psychology* 2 (1974), pp. 128–47.

39. Ibid., p. 153.

40. Kenneth Ring, "Mapping the Regions of Consciousness: A Conceptual Reformulation," *Journal of Transpersonal Psychology* 8, no. 2 (1976), p. 80.

41. Kenneth Wilber, "A Developmental View of Consciousness," *Journal of Transpersonal Psychology* 11, no. 1 (1979), p. 2.

42. Ibid., pp. 12–17.

43. Roberto Assagioli, *Psychosynthesis* (New York: Viking Press, 1965), pp. 17–19.

44. Roberto Assagioli, "Jung and Psychosynthesis," *Journal of Humanistic Psychology* 14, no. 1 (Winter 1974), p. 40.

45. Napoleon Hill, *Think and Grow Rich* (Greenwich, Connecticut: Fawcett Publications, 1963), pp. 67, 197–98.

46. Ibid., p. 72.

47. Charles Bristol, *The Magic of Believing* (New York: Pocket Books, 1948).

48. Ibid., pp. 44–45.

49. Ibid., pp. 45–46.

50. Ibid., p. 47.

51. Agnes Sanford, *The Healing Light* (St. Paul, Minnesota: Macalester Park Publishing Co., 1947), p. 41.

52. *Science Digest* (February 1982), p. 116.

53. Michael Crampton, "Answers From the Unconscious," *Synthesis* 1, no. 2 (1975), pp. 140–52.

54. Charles Baudouin, *Suggestion and Autosuggestion* (London: George Allen & Unwin Ltd., 1954), p. 129.

55. Frederick Myers, *Science and a Future Life* (London: Macmillan & Co., 1893), pp. 36ff.

56. David Klein, *The Unconscious: Invention or Discovery?* (Santa Monica, California: Goodyear Publishing Co., 1977), pp. 82–83.

57. Ibid., p. 78.

58. Ernest White, *Christian Life and the Unconscious* (New York: Harper Brothers, 1955), p. 173.

59. Ibid., p. 172.

60. O. Hobart Mowrer, "Changing Conceptions of the Unconscious," *Journal of Nervous and Mental Disease* 129 (1959), p. 226.

61. O. Hobart Mowrer, "The Unconscious Re-examined in a Religious Context," in *Psychology and Religion,* ed. O. Strunk (New York: Abington Press, 1959), p. 249.

62. Ibid., p. 249.

63. O. Hobart Mowrer, "The Unconscious Re-Examined in a Religious Context," in *The Crises in Psychiatry and Religion* (New York: D. van Nostrand Co., 1961), p. 29.

64. O. Hobart Mowrer, "Communication, Conscience, and the Unconscious," *Journal of Communication Disorders* 1 (1967), p. 110.

65. Morton Kelsey, *God, Dreams, and Revelation* (Minneapolis, Minnesota: Augsburg Publishing House, 1968), pp. ix, 226.

66. Ibid., p. 14.

67. Norman S. Goldman, "An Investigation into a Rabbinic Understanding of Yezar-Ha-Rah and the Unconscious," unpublished D. Min. theses, Eastern Baptist Theological Seminary, 1979, p. 196. Also, "Rabbinic Theology and the Unconscious," *Journal of Religion and Health* 17, no. 2 (1978), pp. 144–50.

Chapter VI

# Final Reflections

## Review of the Opening Material

This investigation of the unconscious opened with the following:
1) questions regarding what the unconscious is; 2) statements concerning the importance of the topic; 3) a list of images of the unconscious; and 4) a list of neologisms given to the unconscious. These items expressed in one form the vastness and complexity of the topic. Without a typological approach, the material alluded to in the above categories is virtually unmanageable. Now that the typology has been presented we can review briefly the opening material and have a better sense of how each item relates to the larger context of the issue of the unconscious.

Regarding the opening series of questions about what the unconscious is we can see now that there is no adequate single answer. As we have reported the construct means different things to different people. The best we can do here is to say that the unconscious, in general, refers to that which influences our behavior, but of which we are unaware. When we try to specify what those influences are we see that it takes a typological approach to answer the question adequately. We have identified four major areas and areas within these that can be considered the sources of various unconscious influences.

Regarding the felt importance of the topic, we agree that it is important. By this we mean that it is very important to study and investigate that which influences our behavior, but of which we are unaware. There is always both danger and promise, fear and expectation, regarding the unknowns of life. On both counts the latter need constant searching into. If the term "unconscious" is used as a short-hand expression of the object of such an exploration, that is, the unknown areas of life, then the term is fine. But, we must remember that whenever it is used in the noun form there is always the danger of it being reified. Warnings not to are of no avail when it is used extensively in this form. Even so, after we have pronounced the word "unconscious," we still have to specify unconscious what? In other words, we have to be specific because the word "unconscious" (noun form) tells us very little. The typological study outlines all the specific areas of the inquiry into the unknown aspects of life that have been conducted in the name of the unconscious. It is these specific areas that are important. The construct of the unconscious has only a very limited value in this endeavor. In fact, we could completely delete the construct and not detract from the importance nor the investigation of the unknown and little-attended-to areas of life. As a matter of observation, investigations into all the specific areas mentioned in this book are going on without being articulated in terms of the construct of the unconscious. This is an inquiry of only those who do, in fact, appeal to the construct.

Although there are many images and metaphors connected to the construct of the unconscious, with the help of the typology, we can make better sense of them. We can identify and appreciate them within the larger context of the topic. Even though many of the images are similar to one another, each one expresses a unique feature of what has been reported about the unconscious. For example, "2,000,000 year old person within us," "storehouse of the wisdom of the ages," "internal guru," and "guardian angel" refer to the life-guiding feature of the unconscious as understood within the transpersonal-spiritual framework. Each metaphor, though, provides a distinct nuance of meaning. Considered altogether, all the images that were cited help us to conjure up a composite sketch of what is subsumed under the term "the unconscious." Some even consider the construct the unconscious itself to be a metaphor—an image standing for something else.

Regarding the neologisms, we have tried to organize them by listing the appropriate ones for each approach in the introduction to the approach. In this way, the original list of approximately eighty terms was subdivided into four main groups. The proliferation of newly coined expressions for one construct has been one of the main reasons for the confusion and controversy surrounding the topic of the unconscious. Why authors have not exercised restraint in this area is a mystery. Common sense would indicate that flooding the verbal market with new terms would only weaken and confuse further the understanding of the construct in question. Sometimes, one gets the impression that theorists want to coin new words.

Notwithstanding what we have just said, there are two possible positive aspects to this condition of many neologisms: 1) the neologisms somehow indicate the felt importance regarding the topic, otherwise no one would bother to offer so many distinctions; 2) the neologisms represent an intent to make needed distinctions involving a very problematic construct. Distinctions are important, but not by taking the originally problematic word and adding adjectives or prefixes to it. As we said in the introduction, if one or any unconscious is still in doubt, the creation of eighty unconsciouses does not advance the discussion, but only compounds the doubts. The distinctions offered in this book are useful in any discussion of the topic. This includes both the major and minor distinctions vis-à-vis each approach. At least they facilitate the understanding and appreciation of the various views.

## Significance of this Book for Psychology

This typological investigation is an explicit statement that the construct of the unconscious is widely and diversely appropriated. It has taken precisely a typological approach to record and organize the different ways the construct is understood. Among the various traditions within psychology the construct of the unconscious is still highly controversial. Some have accepted the construct wholeheartedly and made it the center feature of their systems of ideas, as for example, psychoanalysis and analytical psychology. Some have rejected the construct outright, as for example, behaviorism and experimental psychology. Others such as humanistic psychology, Adlerian psychology, and object relations psychology have redefined the construct to suit their own purposes. In short, the construct of the unconscious has had an unsettled status among the disciplines of psychology.

We have outlined in detail the magnitude of the problem involving one construct and many ways to look at it. It is understandable why the problem of the unconscious is a problem. One can imagine the misunderstandings that can occur when representatives of different approaches convene to discuss some topic in which the construct of the unconscious is used. This is especially so if they are not aware that they represent a distinct approach. The representatives would tend to believe that their own understanding is the most correct and not tend to be aware of the problem of approaches and types involved regarding the construct of the unconscious. How could they do otherwise since there has never been a comprehensive statement of the type problem? This situation does not only happen when people convene to talk, but is also prevalent in the literature on the topic. Authors reveal little awareness of the complexity of the subject matter. It is the intent of this investigation to be of service toward the greater understanding between different points of view by making an explicit statement of the approaches and types involved.

What is to be said about the term "unconscious" itself? We have noted throughout the book the distinctive noun, adverbial, and adjectival usages of the word. We want now to determine how explanatory the construct of the unconscious is for psychology as the science of human behavior. What is to be done with the word "unconscious," especially the noun form usage of it? As we said earlier the adjectival and adverbial usages of the term present no problems and, in fact, there are more descriptive words that could be used. It is the noun form that is problematic. Should psychologists continue to use it or not? Before we answer this question let us consider some salient points.

In the past, various investigators of human behavior, for varying interest, or due to the prevailing interest of their time, have studied different sets of experience. Each of these theorists has assigned a construct of the unconscious to account for the experiences in question. It was the escalation of this practice of assigning agency to the unconscious in order to explain apparently unaccountable behavior that has resulted in the problem of the unconscious.

The existence of any unconscious is not decided by direct inspection. It is an inference that one may draw based the observation of certain behaviors. The unconscious is not discovered per se but inferred, and it is inferred by those who want to infer it. Although it is a temptation rarely and barely overcome *not* to assign a special agency for actions that one cannot easily account for, the existence of the unconscious is not self-evident and the hypothesis of an unconscious is not the only option open to us to account for behavior. How adequate the hypothesis of the unconscious is in explaining behavior depends on who is being asked to accept it.

Although the unconscious is not open to direct inspection, experiences, behavior, and phenomena are open to inspection. We have enumerated the experiences, and so forth, that have been associated with a construct of the unconscious or have been account for in terms of some construct of the unconscious. It is by the process of deescalation, that is, a process of tracing the construct back to the original experiences that gave rise to it and removing its assignment to them that we can untangle step by step the confusion surrounding the construct of the unconscious.

In general, throughout the book we have suggested that the hypothesis of an unconscious to account for experiences, although understandable, is not necessary. It is not the only or the most obvious or logical option open to us to explain certain phenomena. Here we have to be careful to distinguish a real gain in meaning from the impression of having answered the problem by explaining a problematic event by some X-factor. Also, any collection of facts can be related and rendered meaningful by more than one theory. In short, a gain in meaning by employing the construct of the unconscious does not make it a necessary construct. In this polemic over the question of meaning, we have favored the more parsimonious explanations, although we admit that to argue the principle of parsimony reveals more our bias than anything else. This bias is that we do not want to multiply entities unnecessarily. Pardon the metaphor but, if Sigmund Freud said that we are not masters of our own house (the "id" is), and Carl Jung proceeded to make it an "open" house crowded with masters (the archetypes), we want now to "clean" house.

How do we propose to clean house regarding the construct of the unconscious? It must be remembered that everything that has been studied, described, and explained in terms of the unconscious can be and has been studied, described, and explained without it. How adequately this has been done of course depends on who is being asked to accept the explanations. Here we can learn from the Bio-Physical Approach.

In the Bio-Physical Approach, we saw that the construct of the unconscious was confused, as one example, with physiological processes. "Physiological processes" itself is a collective expression that represents the aggregate of, say, processes A, B, C such as subception, autonomic activity, and conditioned reflexes. We begin with and ultimately we have to deal with A, B, and C, which refer to something specific and can be inspected. The expression "physiological processes" tells us very little except to point us in a general direction. Now, to simply attach a construct of the unconscious to refer to physiological processes, as if to imply that the former is an agent responsible for the latter, is at best redundant and at worst mystifying. For these reasons, we said that the construct of the unconscious is unnecessary in the Bio-Physical Approach. It is contended that the same kind of analysis can be conducted regarding the other approaches, and we can come to the same conclusion. We will do this next.

In light of what we have just said, we can look at the four approaches of the typology and observe: 1) in the Bio-Physical Approach, the construct of the unconscious has been used to account for phenomena A, B, C (specified earlier); 2) in the Psycho-Personal Approach, to account for D, E, and F, such as, dream symbolism, forgotten memories, and autonomous complexes; 3) in the Socio-Cultural Approach, to account for G, H, and I, such as, the singular behavior of individuals in groups, the universality of certain symbolic expressions, and certain dimensions of social evils; and 4) in the

Transpersonal-Spiritual Approach, to account for, J, K, and L, such as, the order in nature, transpersonal experiences, and certain paranormal powers. The result has been confusion regarding what the expression "the unconscious" refers to. In each approach area, the construct mystifies more than explains; that is, it covers up our ignorance regarding the experiences in question.

In order to reverse the process by which the construct has been confused, we need to go back to the original experiences such as A, B, C, . . . L. When we do this we see that the construct of the unconscious is really unnecessary. At one point, it may have seemed that the construct was necessary, but we contend that now it is not. It is perceived by many that it only compounds the problems when someone introduces problematic terms to account for already problematic experiences. What this means is that we need more and better understanding about the experiences rather than more words (labels) for them. Giving the unknown a name does not make it less unknown but only gives the impression that we have explained something. The construct of the unconscious has been used to manage that impression.

We can now answer our original question about what to do about the expression "the unconscious." We contend that it should be avoided if possible and qualified if used. It is important that the various fields of psychology continue to study that which influences our behavior, but of which we are not aware, but they need not conduct such inquiries in terms of or in the name of the unconscious. Very little is lost if we put aside this problematic notion. If it continues to be used though, a typological understanding of it is imperative in order to minimize the sources of confusion.

The following tangential comments have to do with other implications of this book for psychology, but are, in a sense, by-products of the investigation.

First, we have assembled a comprehensive body of statements about the numerous variables of human behavior that operate outside the ordinary field of consciousness. We could have entitled this book "The Unconsious Factors of Human Behavior." We could have rewritten it without ever using the word "unconscious" in any form, and still have a substantial contribution for the examination of human behavior.

Second, we have conducted our inquiry according to a four-factor analytic. We have tried to be as comprehensive as possible. In presenting this methodology of approaching the topic in terms of four dimensions, we have suggested:

1. An image of the human being in terms of four dimensions (we have the beginnings of a four-dimensional theory of personality),

2. An approach to psychotherapy which recognizes four main areas that can contribute to a patient's problem (the person is received within a very broad context),

3. A paradigm with which to analyze most experiences, events, and phenomena (these are immediately approached in terms of four dimensions).

Finally, this last ramification of the typological approach relates to a need that has been expressed in the literature. It has been expressed in three forms. It has been written that, "In fact, the idea of the unconscious . . . can acquire scientific status only after a unified picture of the human organism has repaired the intellectual lesions created by Cartesian and other dualistic or specialized methods."[1] In another place it was expressed that "despite numerous attempts, no one has yet succeeded in constructing an integral theory to explain the mechanisms and structure of the unconscious."[2] In still another place it is written that "it is remarkable that no authoritative critical study has yet been made of all ideas of the unconscious from earliest times to the present."[3] This typological investigation is neither the developed integral theory, nor the unified picture, nor the historical study; but it is a foundation for them.

## The Unconscious and Religious Studies

This section will present the state of the psychology of the unconscious vis-à-vis religious and also theological matters. We will also suggest what the construct of the unconscious can represent from a religious and theological point of view. The religionists and theologians need to be informed on both counts.

The psychology of the unconscious is a house divided against itself when it comes to religion. What this means is that there are generally two schools of thought regarding religious experience, and both schools make use of the construct of the unconscious. By religious experiences we are referring to mystical experiences, supernatural phenomena, and experiences with the spiritual world.

We will call one school of thought the reductionist one. Representatives of this point of view do not believe in the vertical nature of religious experiences and seek to reduce them to only psychological and physical terms. The other school of thought will be referred to as the transpersonal school. Advocates of this position accept the possibility of the vertical nature of religious experiences. They accept the existence of a transpersonal dimension. They acknowledge the physical and psychological component of certain experiences, but do not find these two categories adequate enough by themselves to account for all that makes up a religious experience. Both schools of thought employ a theory of the unconscious. We can say that Sigmund Freud is the "schoolmaster" of the reductionist school, and Carl Jung the "schoolmaster" of the transpersonal one.

The contrast between the two schools is made explicit by the following two lists composed by Paul Johnson.[4] He compared Freud and Jung on the question of religious experiences.

| Freud saw religious experiences in these terms: | Jung saw them in these: |
|---|---|
| regression | progression |
| illusion | revelation |
| neurotic | therapeutic |
| repressive | releasing |
| motivated by guilt | motivate by growth |
| obsessive | purposive |
| evasive | invasive |
| reductive | productive |
| egocentric | outgoing through enlarging relationships |

These two lists also apply to the two schools to which we alluded. The key point here is that the sets of categories are derived from two different understanding of what the unconscious is and how it operates in one's life. In terms of the typology, the reductionist school subsumes the Psycho-Personal Approach and some aspects of the Bio-Physical. The transpersonal school is directly related to the Transpersonal-Spiritual Approach. We will say more about the reductive school and then discuss the other one.

Although we referred metaphorically to Freud as the master of the reductionist school, his ideas are not the only ones that support this point of view. We would like to present two other points of view in addition to Freud's.

Freud made no secret of his program to translate metaphysics into metapsychology. He confidently stated that one day the psychology of the unconscious, as he envisioned it, would replace mythological conceptions and all talk of transcendental realities.[5] For him, any and all religious (and even para-psychological) experiences could be accounted for in terms of impulses, disguised wishes, and their vicissitudes. All of this is negotiated by the unconscious. The psychic system is a closed one, and the motto here is "nothing from without." Religious experiences began, transpired, and ended within this closed system.

Let us consider another expression of the reductionist mode, this time from a representative of the Bio-Physical Approach. He is Julian Jaynes. Jaynes bases his speculations on the findings of left-right brain research. Essentially, he suggested that what a person once heard and believed to be the voice of God, was, in reality, the "voice" of the right hemisphere. Jaynes went on the explain:

> There is some vestigial functioning of the right Wernicke's area (in the right hemisphere) in a way similar to the voices of gods. The experimental foundation of this point involved the stimulation of the Wernicke's area and subjects reporting that they heard voices . . . the important thing about almost all these stimulation caused experiences is their otherness, their opposition from the self, rather than the self's own actions or own words.[6]

Here we have another "nothing from without" theory, but this time based on a bio-physical foundation. Jaynes' highly speculative hypothesis suggests that the brain itself manages the impression of transcendence in order to command the authority necessary to direct the actions of men.

The final example we will consider could be identified within the Transpersonal-Spiritual Approach. As we shall soon see, there is more irony here than contradiction. We are referring to the ideas of D. H. Rawcliffe. Rawcliffe entertained a construct of the subconscious mind. He rejected the idea of considering mind or subconscious mind as entities. For him, the latter expression was a collective term for all mental activity that lies below the level of consciousness.

He described three features of this subconscious mind: 1) that it could perform subconsciously those routine jobs requiring little or no originality; in fact, it could perform several activities simultaneously; 2) that it never ceases to function from the day one is born until death; and 3) that, under special conditions, it possesses independent powers, not only of imagination and fantasy such as in dreams, but also of reasoning and intelligence equal and sometimes superior to conscious mental activity.[7] There is nothing transpersonal about this subconscious mind. He limited it to what we have called the bio-physical and psycho-personal dimensions. This point is crucial to Rawcliffe's plan to rationally explain (really explain away) every paranormal experience. After all, he entitled his book *Illusions and Delusions of the Supernatural and the Occult.*

Rawcliffe defined four notions, namely, subconscious mind, mental dissociation, suggestion, and hysteria. With these he proceeded to account for such phenomena as stigmata, ghosts, seances, firewalking, mystical experiences, visions, auras, levitation, lycanthropy, healing, automatic writing, and voices. His accounts are interesting and sometimes forced exercises in pure rationalism, and his demonstrations and conclusions are suggestive at best. Here is the point about the irony involved. He should not have used the expression "subconscious mind" the way he did because, even though he issued a warning not to reify it, he gave an air of mystery to the construct, and it did appear to function like an entity. He created more mystery in his strained efforts to remove the mystery related to certain phenomena.

In sum, what we have with Freud, Jaynes, and Rawcliffe are three ways a reductionist analytic can be shaped using three distinct theories of what the unconscious is. What are we to make of this reductive approach?

For one, it is not really a new approach, but a new expression of an old approach. This time it happens to appear in the form of the psychology of the unconscious. The old, but ever-present argument is that God, religion, and all spiritual phenomena are only the creations of people. It was in Greece, around 300 B.C., that Euhemerus contended that the gods were really deified persons. Today, Freud has refined the argument to say that God is really a deified, that is, an introjected, sublimated or compensated, and projected father figure. This illusion is managed by the unconscious, in the service of a wish, in the service of an impulse, in the service of *soma*.

To call an argument old though does not really refute it. Two things can be said here. One, in general the argument that religion is the product of only human factors is understandable given that some do not believe in spiritual or religious phenomena. After all, if one excludes a transpersonal-spiritual dimension from consideration, what choice has one other than to find meaning in terms of bio-physical, psycho-personal, and socio-cultural realities.

The second point involves the construct of the unconscious. To the extent that the reductionist argument is based on and articulated in terms of a psychology of the unconscious it is a weak argument. We made the point explicitly in second section of this chapter that the hypothesis of the unconscious is not necessary although legitimate. Ironically, the way the construct is used sometimes is just as superstitious as the reductionists claim that the constructs of God, soul, spirit, and so forth, appear to them.

On the posivite side there is something that we can learn from a psychology of the unconscious in the service of reductionism. We are aware of the fact that there are human motivational factors and foundations for religious experiences. Sometimes, though, we may underestimate this component of the experiences. Because the ideas of those who represent the reductionist mode are limited to only bio-physical and psycho-personal dimensions, those who entertain these ideas can function like devil's advocates vis-à-vis the person who has had a religious experience. In a sense, this can represent a test of faith and a challenge to go beyond the oedipal foundations of one's commitment to a religion so that the commitment is based on more than the desire for security and the fear of punishment. Spiritual directors and religious counselors, today, who are aware of this mode of the psychology of the unconscious, can perform a function similar to what spiritual directors did in the past in what the mystical tradition called the purgative stage of ascent toward holiness. This is not to say that they cannot do this without a psychology of the unconscious, but merely to point out that they could make use of it in this way. In sum, the psychology of the unconscious in the reductionist mode is both a challenge to the faith and a means to purify it. But, as stated earlier, to the extent that it reifies the construct of the unconscious, it is itself on uncertain ontological ground.

Now, let us turn to the transpersonal school. We can refer back to the entire fifth chapter, which involved the Transpersonal-Spiritual Approach. Everyone mentioned there is part of this school of thought. In that approach, we presented ideas such as the intelligence in nature, varieties of transpersonal experiences, special powers claimed to be performed by the unconscious, and contact with the spiritual world.

The key point here is the fact that every single fact, experience, and phenomenon mentioned within the Transpersonal-Spiritual Approach, before the word "unconscious" was coined (around 1750), was understood in terms of the following categories: God, soul, angels, demons, spirits, or Spirit. These were the terms available and used by religious people when they needed to assign an agent or cause to some otherwise unexplainable event. In this observation, we have a clue to what the construct of the unconscious represents. We contend that, in the service of the transpersonal approach, the construct of the unconscious represents the secular search for God, meaning, and the spiritual dimension of life.

The unconscious is in some cases the secular answer offered as an alternative to the theological list of possible agents operating in human beings and in the world. This point is very evident in the Romantic tradition that we discussed in the Transpersonal-Spiritual Approach, and we have Eduard von Hartmann's own words to support this contention. He wrote that "it seems to me advisable to avoid as far as possible in philosophy an idea with an origin so exclusively religious as God. I shall therefore continue as a rule to employ the expression 'The Unconscious' . . . Although the formal negativity of my terminology for an out-and-out positive Being must for a length of time be inadequate, yet it will retain its proper prophylactic value as long as the anthropopathic error of the consciousness of the Absolute prevails to a considerable extent . . . hopefully later a more appropriate and positive term will be found."[8]

It is not difficult to liken the *Summa Theologica* of Thomas Aquinas to the quasi-"Summa" of von Hartmann. Aquinas, among other things, attempted to account for many experiences such as fate, daemon, rapture, divination, inspiration, prophecy, dreams, and coincidences by using the constructs God, soul, spirits, and so forth. Today someone has associated all of these items with some theory of the unconscious.

Hartmann, too, wrote a voluminous work attempting to account for many experiences. He began with what he termed The Unconscious and proceeded to show how everything is derived and sustained by this Being. This is more than an interesting parallel; it is an attempt to offer an alternative understanding to the orthodox theological one. This alternative began to be offered in the same century that the word "unconscious" was coined, and has found its way into the twentieth century in the form of the construct of the Objective Psyche, which is promoted by the Jungians.

How are we to respond to the transpersonal approach as we have described? In some respects, our answer is shaped in the same manner as that given to the reductionist analytic. First, it is understandable that those who believe in spiritual phenomena as such would be dissatisfied with explanations that exclude a transpersonal-spiritual dimension. Also, some do not accept the orthodox theological constructs. It seems that the construct of the unconscious serves on both counts.

Second, as we said about the reductionist analytic so too with the transpersonal one; that is, it is not a new approach but a new form of an old idea. Again, we can go back to the early Greeks. We can trace some of the features of the Romantic construct of the unconscious back through the panentheistic tradition all the way back to Anaxagoras' (fifth century B.C.) notion of *Nous*. This was speculated to be a shaping mind acting in the ordering of matter and independent of it. There are even some traces of the Stoic notion of *Logos,* especially in terms of its being related to a world-soul idea. We should note here that the panentheistic tradition has found its way into Western theological systems; for example, as early as the ninth century with the ideas of Eurigena, and, in our century, in the form of process theology.

The early Fathers of Christianity used the Greek ideas in their apologetic efforts with the non-Christians. Maybe today's theologian can use the construct of the unconscious in the same spirit. The argument is not hard to imagine. We have already alluded to it. We said that what secular sources try to account for in terms of the unconscious (in a transpersonal-spiritual context), the theologian and religionist have always articulated in terms of God, soul, spirit, and so forth.

It is the intent of this book to investigate and determine the substance of this secular answer known as the unconscious. We concluded that the unconscious is not necessarily any thing, and that the expression really functions as an X-factor. If nothing else, it does represent the modern and secular symbol for the unknown and ineffable aspects of life. What this means is that the religionist ought to recognize that implicit in the construct of the unconscious is a person's search for the ultimate ground of the phenomenon of human behavior.

The religionist and the theologian ought to understand well this construct of the unconscious as a symbol for a person's search for Ultimate Reality. Toward this better understanding the typology can be of service. It provides a very broad context within which to

entertain ideas articulated in terms of the construct of the unconscious, and allows for distinctions to be made in efforts toward con-
structive criticism, apologetics, and positive theological-psychologi-
cal synthesis. Also, when the theologian hears, for example, the
Jungian advice that the twentieth-century theologian ought to know
about the unconscious in order to reach twentieth-century people,
the theologian can take that advice in its fullest meaning without
necessarily having to accept the Jungian system of ideas about the
unconscious. In other words, the religionist and the theologian, with
the help of the typology, are free to speculate about the construct of
the unconscious in any of the many ways of understanding it without
feeling that one must accept any particular interpretation. One also
learns about the intricate matrix of subtle factors that influence
human motivation and behavior without having to necessarily accept
any construct of the unconscious. If one chooses to accept some such
construct, one knows how to distinguish it. Finally, the typology
insures that the transpersonal-spiritual perspective will be recognized
as one major source of input within the larger universe or discourse on
the topic of the unconscious.

## The Future of the Unconscious

There are many factors that could conceivably influence the future
direction and nature of the study of the unconscious. We want to
consider here two significant factors that have been and continue to
be important. We are referring to the models and the state of the
sciences. Theories of the unconscious have been directly influenced
by these things.

For example, Freud's theory was influenced by the hydraulic and
electrical models and terms of physics in his time. There are other
examples. The concept of the gradient in biology encouraged some,
as for example Rex Collier, to understand the conscious-unconscious
relationship as a continuum rather than as a dichotomous one.[9] Karl
Pribram's holographic theory allowed some, such as Ernest Rossi, to
speculate about a holographically functioning unconscious mind.[10]
Systems theory led to systems theories of the mind and the uncon-

scious. We saw an example of this discussed within the Socio-Cultural Approach (see pages 105–107). The development of mathematical symbolic logic allowed Ignacio Matte-Blanco to write about the unconscious as infinite sets.[11]

Even the state of a science in terms of its technology has been an influence. For example, in 1846 Carl Carus wrote his book *Psyche* after having been able to look into a microscope, which had just come into use. He constructed the entire argument of his book based on the conclusions he drew from what he thought he saw in the microscope. Today, computer technology dominates, and it is no surprise that someone would conceive the psyche to be like a computer. For example, Charles Tart referred to the biological givens of a person as "hardware" and referred to those structures given by a particular developmental history as "software." Tart pictured the relationship among the psychic structures as subsystems comprising states of consciousness and following feedback routes. One of these subsystems, he called the subconscious, which contains a curious mixture of Freudian, Jungian, and other features.[12]

Another modern example relates to left-right brain research. Some, such as David Galin, have suggested that the unconscious may be a right-brain based phenomenon. This model has come about because of recent developments in brain surgery and the development of the electronic hardware that goes along with brain studies. We might add here that certain epileptic patients were also an integral part of the development of this model. Indeed, the patient factor has also been significant throughout the history of many theories of personality as well as theories of the unconscious.

It is probable that the computer and right-left brain models will continue to influence the way we understand ourselves. It is not uncommon to hear someone described as being "programed," or someone to remark about a couple that they are a perfect "right and left brain" match. If the construct of the unconscious is associated with this way of thinking, it will no doubt be articulated in terms of these models. Whether it is these models or others, the future discussion and study of the topic of the unconscious will be tied to the vicissitudes of models and the advances in the state of the sciences.

Given the complexity of the topic of the unconscious, the vast array of experiences it is presumed to account for, and the inherent, direct unapproachability of what it refers to, it is entirely fitting that we make use of metaphors, images, models, and analogies. It ought to be kept in mind though that the experiences the construct of the unconscious is called in to explain are still being investigated for answers and many experiences are highly controversial topics. In other words the construct of the unconscious has not substantially advanced our understanding regarding certain phenomena. Although not really an explanation the construct at least remains as a symbol for the subtle and little-known factors of human behavior.

# Notes

1. Lancelot Whyte, "Unconscious," *Encyclopedia of Philosophy,* ed. Paul Edwards (New York: Macmillan and Free Press, 1967), p. 185.

2. A. M. Prokhorov, ed. "Unconscious," *The Great Soviet Encyclopedia* (New York: Macmillan, 1976), p. 772.

3. Whyte, *Encyclopedia of Philosophy,* p. 188.

4. Paul Johnson, "Unconscious Motivation," in *Psychology and Religion* (New York: Abingdon Press, 1959), pp. 203–12.

5. Sigmund Freud, "Determinism, Chance, and Superstitious Belief," in *The Psychopathology of Everyday Life* (New York: Macmillan Co., n.d.), pp. 309–10.

6. Julian Jaynes, *The Origin of Consciousness and the Breakdown of the Bicameral Mind* (Boston: Houghton Mifflin Co., 1976), pp. 106–108. Jaynes did not write in terms of the unconscious, but, to the extent that the right hemisphere has been speculated to be the place of the unconscious, we can include his ideas here.

7. D. H. Rawcliffe, *Illusions and Delusions of the Supernatural and the Occult* (New York: Dover Publications, Inc., 1959).

8. Eduard von Hartmann, *The Philosophy of the Unconscious* (London: Routledge and Kegan Paul, 1950), p. 275.

9. Rex Collier, "A Figure-Ground Model Replacing the Conscious-Unconscious Dichotomy," *Journal of Individual Psychology* 20 (1964), pp. 3–16.

10. Ernest L. Rossi, "As Above, So Below: The Holographic Mind," *Psychological Perspective* 11, no. 2 (Fall 1980), pp. 155–69.

11. Ignacio Matte-Blanco, *The Unconscious As Infinite Set* (New York: Duckworth, 1975).

12. Charles Tart, "Discrete States of Consciousness," in *Symposium on Consciousness,* edited by Philip Lee et al, (New York: Viking Press, 1976), p. 130.

# Index

167